Public Education and Day Care

PUBLIC EDUCATION AND DAY CARE

one district's story

CAROL M. HOFFMAN, **M.Ed.**

TECHNOMIC
PUBLISHING CO., INC.

Technomic Publishing Company, Inc.
851 New Holland Avenue
Box 3535
Lancaster, Pennsylvania 17604

Cover Illustration by Michael Deraco
Cover Lettering by Bobby Deraco

Printed in the United States of America

10 9 8 7 6 5 4 3 2 1

Main entry under title:
  Public Education and Day Care: One District's Story

A Technomic Publishing Company book
Bibliography: p. 105

Library of Congress Card No. 84-52676
ISBN No. 87762-389-9

TO
DR. STANLEY T. DUBELLE, JR.
SUPERINTENDENT
WILSON SCHOOL DISTRICT
WEST LAWN, PA

Monetary proceeds
from the sale of this book
will be placed in a fund
to be used for
the Wilson School District's
Early Childhood Program,
especially toward
salary increases and inservice offerings
for day care staff.

CONTENTS

FOREWORD

The Day Care movement in the United States is an unstoppable force. The need and demand for child care services continues to grow faster than statisticians can rework their figures. Each new week brings with it a new set of numbers. Each new set of numbers brings with it a new set of anxieties.

The person most affected on a long-term basis by this need for child care is today's child, yet the person least understood or seriously considered is the child himself . . . the child herself.

More than half of this country's mothers work at jobs outside the home. Most one-parent homes are headed by a woman, although a significant number of fathers is emerging as the only parent in the home. One consequence of the changing American family is a demand for child care services.

Like it or not, day care is here to stay—at least in my lifetime. Wishing it would disappear does nothing to improve the quality of this phenomenon of the century. Day Care is a snowball running rampant. We weren't ready for it when it commenced rolling during World War II. We weren't ready for it when it plowed through our quiet little towns and valleys after having overtaken the cities.

Day Care is now everywhere. What do we do with this

"thing" that has obviously become too big to handle properly?

It is reasonable to say that public education needs to step in and redirect the movement. Where day care is succeeding through loving, child-oriented private or public programs, public education should agree on a hands-off policy.

Wherever day care is *not* the best for children and their parents, perhaps public education ought to step in and offer alternative, high-quality programs.

Pie in the sky?

Worming our way in where we don't belong?

Taking over the responsibility of parents and families?

Taking over the role of the church?

Biting off more than we can chew?

Obviously, you can come up with a few more phrases intended to block your efforts to blaze a new trail for public education.

We've heard them all. For several years, these phrases were semi-effective in thwarting my efforts to pursue day care in the public school. These phrases slowed me down until I began visiting some badly operated private day care centers. These phrases slowed me down until I saw what I perceived as long-term negative effects on the children.

Children who may be hurt—or are hurting—cannot be ignored. Public education has to care about what's happening.

This handbook is the outgrowth of five years of intensive day care study. As a result, it is the story of one public school district's belief in and commitment to establishing a day care center for its children.

Thanks to the Wilson School District's administrators and Board of Education members, the data will be permitted to flow honestly, candidly, and in an unvarnished way—just the way it happened.

What's more, this handbook is being written in plain English and in very practical, readable terms.

We want this handbook to be useful to anyone wishing to explore the day care concept in the public school.

We want this handbook to be useful to public educators who are interested in meeting the myriad developmental needs of today's child.

Today's child brings with him a whole set of new complexities. A school district that opens caring arms to children before they begin formal education is a district with a head start on meeting the immediate and long-term needs of today's little ones.

Today's child is a "hurried" child. Read David Elkind's insightful work. Nobody says it better than Elkind.

Today's child is often "overplaced" by one grade during his school career. Read the works of the Gesell Institute educators. Nobody studies developmental overplacement better than they do.

Today's child is asked to handle concepts that are way beyond her developmental grasp. Read and reread Jean Piaget's theories. Nobody observes and synthesizes better than this Swiss thinker.

Today's child is asked to handle adult themes during the preschool years and then emerge emotionally and socially healthy. Read Erik Erikson's work on Psycho-social development and feel a little scared about what we're doing to kids *before* they enter school. Erikson paints the trust and esteem picture better than anybody else even though he never had day care in mind when developing his theories.

Today's very young child is not understood *holistically* or from a developmental point-of-view. Among others, read Burton White's book, *The First Three Years* and absorb the life-long significance of those formative years. White believes what he writes as staunchly as anyone else in the field.

Today's child is not understood within the context of family or "group." Read the works of Rudolf Dreikurs, Haim Ginott, Urie Bronfenbrenner, James Dobson, or Fitzhugh

Dodson. As professional observers of human behavior, they perceive, with accurate sensitivity, the child within the family.

Today's child. Who is truly raising today's child?

How is today's child being nurtured?

What do the fragmented family and the day care movement mean to human growth and development?

These major questions are among the many we will be exploring, because . . . this book is about today's child.

Specifically, it is about a fact of life for many of today's children. This fact of life is day care.

Acknowledgments

A page or two must be reserved for all the Wilson School District people who have directly influenced the success of our day care program. Listing names is risky because certainly more people than we name here have been contributors.

Dr. Stanley T. Dubelle remains first on this list because he believed before he saw. Without his trust and commitment, Wilson's Day Care Program wouldn't be more than an idea whose time still hasn't arrived. Public education becomes more viable whenever educationally sound ideas are allowed to be born and nurtured. Public educators like Stan are always controversial. Fortunately, he has the courage to listen, believe, and act on those beliefs. He is committed to excellence in public education, and I wouldn't want to be associated with leaders who aren't visibly, actively committed to excellence. It is no secret that I believe Stan is the best total educator I have ever met. Although his mental energy can be overwhelming at times, to me he is Teacher, colleague, and friend.

Lee Fredericks provided a solid emotional and informational base as we pursued the idea of day care. Lee is Wilson's Assistant Superintendent. He is a low-key, capable, quietly caring listener as well as a strong advocate of early childhood education. I respect Lee and am grateful for his helpful ways.

The Board of Education that sanctioned our program is made up of the following caring people:

Verne C. Bausher	Alan K. Raffauf *(Retired)*
Geraldine S. Cook *(Retired)*	Glenn B. Reber *(Retired)*
Alan W. Hohl	Jean A. Seelicke
Marilyn S. Kershner, M.D.	David E. Seifert
Terry L. Mancini	Beverly A. Snyder
Anthony A. Matz, Jr. *(Retired)*	Conrad D. Wagner *(Retired)*
Thomas W. Ott	George R. Wissler

While a few of us have been the dreamers and planners, the following are the doers:

Whitfield Center	Lincoln Park Center
Jennifer Kell,	Karen Zerbe,
Group Supervisor	*Group Supervisor*
Joyce Boutros	Justine Barbitta
Margery DaDamio	Bonita Goshert
Barbara Messner	Sherri McConomy
	Ann Ritter

Our four Elementary Principals also earned our thanks. They are Joseph Charnigo, Marjorie Miller, Niles Stoudt, and Joseph Toy.

Secretaries have a way of emerging as unsung heroines. Our secretaries are no exception. These special, helpful people are Lisa DeLong, Neda Mae Wert, Esther Kowalski, and Hazel Kunkel.

Doug Houston, Wilson's Business Manager, came to our rescue on a number of occasions. His cheerful perseverance in handling the nuts and bolts things like insurance, refrigerators, and furniture moving and repair, deserves several hugs.

Ann Worley, Home Economics Teacher, oversees our high school volunteer program. As a result, thirty high school students spend a school year involved in day care. A big thanks to Ann.

The person who has worked closest to our day care program on a daily basis is Mary Long. Since 1981, Mary has been the rock of Wilson's Early Childhood Program. It is no understatement to say she has been—and continues to be—a valuable assistant in all our projects. Unassuming, intelligent, warm, and skillfully efficient, Mary is "always there." For all you do and are, Mary, thanks.

And to those whose names do not appear, please feel good about your own special contribution to the Wilson School District's Day Care Program.

Who Is Raising America's Children?

The title of our opening chapter ought to be "Frank." Oh, not Frank as in Sinatra, but frank as in candid, unvarnished, blunt. It is written to enlighten, not enrage. It is written to encourage thinking, not emotional reaction. It is written to educate professional educators as well as parents and child care employees.

Day Care is everybody's concern. Sooner or later the way we are raising America's children will affect all of us. Because the way we care for our children during their waking hours *matters* to all of society, "Frank" is the real title of this chapter.

And as we go on, do not be surprised if we become even "Franker."

Between 55 and 60 percent of America's mothers of young children work at jobs outside the home. If we are to believe statistics, then most of today's parents are sharing the raising of their children with an assortment of strangers, an older child, a relative, and, occasionally, a neighbor or friend. Children whose mothers work full-time outside the home spend more waking hours with an assortment of adults other than mother. Children whose only parent is father also spend most of their waking hours with other adults. There are, of course, exceptions. In a few cases, mothers and fathers are creatively employed and are able to

1

take their children along to work. However, *most* parents employed outside the home need child care services.

We don't need statistics, a calculator, or a master's degree in mathematics in order to figure out the number of hours today's preschoolers are spending away from parents. This "amount of time" issue is such an emotional one, most parents and educators tend publicly to avoid it. For the last decade, we have been tip-toeing around sensitive topics rather than dealing with them head-on. Well, it is this educator's opinion that we have created problems by *not* looking at a social issue as it truly exists.

It is irrefutable that a mother who works 35 to 40 hours a week outside the home during her child's waking hours *won't* be caring *for* her child those hours. I did not say she won't be caring *about* her child. There's a big difference.

Critical-about-day-care adults need to see this difference just as overly-sensitive-to-criticism employed mothers (or single fathers) need to see this difference. Until both human sides of this sensitive issue can sit down and share facts as well as needs and emotions, we'll get nowhere. That's why we've been getting nowhere for decades!

Public educators interested in establishing child care programs need to be aware of—and ready for—the defensive or hostile responses of a number of parents who seek day care for their children. Likewise, parents, sometimes caught in the emotional guilt web of the "working parent," need to be aware of—and ready for—societal criticism, including criticism from educators. There is no escaping conflict. It exists. It will not go away soon or expeditiously. It can only be eased by examining the total issue in mutually respectful ways.

Let's look at several ways we can respectfully and logically examine Who Is Raising America's Children?

First of all, we can survey our own community. The census may be a starting place. The school may be another. Churches or agencies are still other sources of information.

Find out *approximately* how many single parents live in your community, how many parents are employed, and how many of these parents have children between the ages of birth and sixth grade.

Next, gather data on the number of day care or child care centers in your community. Discover approximately how many children are being cared for in these centers. Ask about fees and services. Ask to visit the facilities. Ask many questions.

At this point, something is happening to you. You discover yourself in a maze of social change that challenges your ability to comprehend and analyze situations. You discover that the *more information* you gather, the less you know about the original question. You also discover that the information you gathered last week is obsolete today. The ever-changing world of day care and child care makes for an elusive study in frustration and incredulity.

Who is raising America's children?

Everybody.

Anybody.

Day care workers who are overworked and underpaid.

Day care workers who are overworked and underqualified.

Day care workers who like children.

Day care workers who can't stand children.

Grandmas, aunts, neighbors, boyfriends, and girlfriends.

Other children.

The television set.

Women or men who operate family day care "homes."

Child care workers in non-profit public programs.

Child care workers in private-for-profit programs.

College graduates who have no understanding of child development.

Non-college graduates who have considerable understanding of child development.

Loving, caring, mentally healthy adults.

Mentally unhealthy adults.

Entrepeneurs with little interest in what's best for children.

Entrepeneurs who care about what's best for children.

Enough is enough. We could fill several pages with our answer to the original question. However, the only valid answer to the question, "Who is raising America's children?" is: A wide variety of people other than, but usually including, parents.

Twenty years ago it would have been easy to answer that question. The complex pattern of day care was not yet so tightly woven, so intricate, so *fragile* . . . so scary.

Citing statistics is an exercise in obsolescence so we will keep our "stats" to a minimum. However, educators and parents need to sense the importance of several current statistics and child care research projects. Educators and parents also need to understand the laws of human growth and development, especially from birth to age ten. The reason we suggest an understanding of the first ten years of life is the fact that a growing majority of children in this age group are spending their waking hours away from their parents. Are the people to whom we trust our children the best kind of people for children? Are they warm, loving, happy, healthy adults? Do they have either "book-learning" in regard to child development or a natural common sense "gift" when it comes to caring for and about children?

Recently, four *major* day care scandals have erupted and emotionally rocked this country in the course of a week. A psychologist assigned to interview several hundred children involved as "victims" of one of the scandals said some important things. During a national television interview, she said exploitation of children in day care centers or babysitters' homes is not at all uncommon. She says sexual abuse, neglect, battering, pornography, and other forms of exploitation of children exist in child care centers in every area of the United States.

With an increase in parents' employment outside the home, we are bound to see an increase in the numbers of "unfit" care givers. We feel bad for the many beautiful care givers out there and exclude them from our concern. While many high quality day care staffs are operating excellent programs for children, we are becoming aware of increasing numbers of child care environments destined to harm the present and future of our children. It is the latter about which we must be "franker."

Educators and parents need to understand that almost anyone can decide to go into the child care business. While Department of Welfare officials would be quick to remind us of licensing requirements, they would also agree that many, many day care providers are escaping these requirements. As a result, hundreds, perhaps thousands, of child care providers are operating in complete freedom, unknown to evaluators and far from the monitoring eye of keen, caring observers. The most frightening implication arising is the *fact* that the latest major child abuse cases took place in *licensed* day care centers in rather affluent communities. What's happening in the less affluent communities? All we can do for the moment is shudder.

The world of day care is an umbrella that gets larger and more unmanageable every day! As a crisis-oriented society, we tend to let things go from bad to worse before we act. As a society we aren't very good at activating the adage "An ounce of prevention is worth a pound of cure." As a society we tend to mimic the ostrich so we don't have to look and see and then do something about our problems.

And so, as a society we are allowing our children to pay for our refusal to take caring, responsible action.

As our children pay, so shall we.

The cost to human worth and dignity is prohibitive, as we are discovering. Yet if we can't or won't rally round kids, around whom will we rally? Who is worth more than our children?

5

If we neither like nor can afford the consequences of the answer to the question, "Who is raising America's children?" what are we prepared to do about it?

Public schools just may be a reliable, trusting partner today's parent so badly needs. While public schools do not have a legal obligation to provide care for preschool children or before and after school care for school-age children, public education may be the natural and logical day care provider.

Child care programs developed by public school districts can operate at no cost to district taxpayers. (The second part of this book is devoted to this subject.)

An expensive problem can become a no-cost-to-schools solution.

The answer to our original question would then be altered somewhat because the school and home would form an early partnership. *Parent's* responsibility for "raising" children would be advocated and parent courses, tips, ideas, workshops, and other forms of practical communication could be developed through the school. Public schools would become a helper to parents, not a replacement.

Consider the many benefits to children if public education opened its arms to the world of day care. The physical and emotional safety of little ones would be almost assured. Staff and programs would be supervised by public school administrators. There would be fewer opportunities for mentally unhealthy adults to join or remain in day care positions if programs are operated by public schools.

Parents might experience a decrease in tension and anxiety if public education became their day care partner. Our Wilson School District day care parents say, "We can depend on you and trust that the kids are in good hands." The dependability–reliability factor is said to be a day care parent's biggest nightmare. Day care centers operated by public schools would be dependable and reliable. They wouldn't open one week and close the next. They wouldn't have to exist on the shaky edge of bankruptcy from month to month. They wouldn't operate as a profit-making business and could, therefore, offer quality child care at relatively low cost to parents.

Public education *itself* might receive a much needed public relations boost by opening those caring arms to day care children. That much needed P.R. boost might be just what public education needs on its way to breathing new life into an aging respiratory system.

Educators can no longer ignore the fact of day care and its consequences. Neither can parents nor the general public.

One educational association, the National Association for the Education of Young Children, has been both vocal yet virtually ignored "outside" in regard to day care needs in the United States. The NAEYC's publication, *Young Children*, is an excellent source of information. Public school educators would find useful, enlightening articles and research data in each issue of *Young Children*. It would be a good starting point in educating educators about day care!

Only recently have nationally known educators planted the seed of marriage between public schools and day care. Dr. Bettye Caldwell, one of this country's best-known early childhood educators, said the following words during her address to the NAEYC Convention in Atlanta on November 6, 1983:

> One of our biggest challenges in terms of linkages is to make peace with the public schools. If you think child care is under seige, just reflect on what public education is experiencing with so many national reports proclaiming everything that is wrong with the schools. Yet, even with an awareness of those problems, I am an advocate of establishing closer linkages with the schools.
>
> For almost ten years I directed the Kramer Project in Little Rock which operated a high quality early childhood program in a public school. Children from 6 months to 12 years of age were enrolled, and the school operated year round from 6:45 a.m. until 6:00 p.m. The elementary teachers did

modify some of their attitudes and ideas about teaching young children. Parents loved the program and found it convenient to have all their children young enough to need continuous supervision in the same program. Now every primary school in Little Rock provides before and after school care.

Public schools are not the enemies of early childhood programs, but if we do not make them aware of us and what we can contribute to the overall development of the children in their programs, they will be less likely to give us the support we need in the development of public policies for children and families. If we want to move out of the domain of pathology which is where we started, an alliance with education may be the most helpful linkage we can establish. That does not mean surrendering to education, but rather exerting influence and sharing public resources.[1]

Public education will find it increasingly more difficult to ignore the day care question. Those public schools whose administrators don blinders and earmuffs may soon pay for their chosen blindness and deafness. As they dig in their heels of avoidance, they may find themselves rattling around *one last year* in near-vacant white elephants that used to be called school buildings.

If public educators don't soon discard blinders and earmuffs, private education and private enterprise will find ways to meet the needs of parents who work outside the home.

It will happen.

It *is* happening.

Because it is happening and we don't know how to react or respond to the situation, we look for people to blame. We blame Democrats, Republicans, Independents, Communists, General Motors, the state of California, television, movies, alcohol, and drugs, but more than any other "group," we tend to blame women.

And that's not only unfair, it's untrue. The day care concept was spawned during World War II . . . and not by women.

When Johnny came marching home, not *all* mothers willingly marched back to the kitchen. Some mothers decided to continue working in the factories and offices and stores. As a result, grandmothers and aunts and neighbors were recruited for child care. The supply of grandmas, aunts, and neighbors initially far outweighed the demand for their services. Only here and there was the day care seed dropped. Quietly, undramatically, the seed grew.

Cities felt growth first. Sputnik and the civil rights movement planted still more seeds. Federal monies multiplied time and again during the 1960's, creating energetic and expensive social and educational programs for America's minorities.

And the most "minority" group of all inherited, unsolicited, the day care concept conceived during World War II. Children are the inheritors.

Today's children—red and yellow, black and white—are fast becoming day care children. In just twenty-five years, the day care phenomenon has crept from city to suburb to town to farm to city to . . . everywhere in the United States.

It is too soon to judge, objectively and empirically, the effects of day care on families, communities, government, and society-at-large. Most of our judgments tend to be emotional or value-based. We either hate the idea of day care or yield to its services when we discover we need those services. Few of us are fence-sitters in regard to our feelings about day care. Still fewer of us are seriously examining the most important day care issue: *the children*!

It may be too soon to judge the effects of day care on families, communities, government, and society-at-large but it surely isn't too soon to judge the effects on children.

The scary part is that if many of us don't soon thoughtfully and intelligently examine consequences to children, we may discover a generation or two or three of Americans who display complex, multiple growth and general life needs.

The question that used to be asked is now obsolete: Should the day care movement continue?

(In case you didn't realize it, the above *question* is now defunct. However, the answer to it is "The day care movement cannot be stopped.")

We need to address viable questions in order to study the effects of day care on children. These questions are:

Who is raising America's children?

How?

What does care away from home mean to the developing mind, body, and emotions?

Public education, more than any other social component, needs to take a more vigorous interest in the phenomenon of day care. Who can better examine day care through unbiased eyes? Educators are only now beginning to perceive the reality of this unstoppable force. As a result, public educators are accepting the idea that they can no longer estrange themselves from the day care issue. Day care and latch key *children* are becoming the majority of their students. Teachers, administrators, and Boards of Education—along with parents—need to care enough to examine those three critical questions. The very existence of public education may be inextricably tied to the *answers*.

Many day care centers are licensed to operate Kindergartens. A child who attends private Kindergarten via day care is a child who is *not* attending public school. It is only a matter of time before enterprising day care center directors begin operating first and second grades as well as providing before and after school care. When (not if) this somewhat iconoclastic movement becomes a fact, public education may be too shocked to pull itself out if its self-imposed swamp. Add to the private first and second grade idea a tuition tax credit program sanctioned by the United States of

America and public education is really in trouble. Two-pronged competition will do one of two things to public schools: awaken them or bury them.

Let's assume public education chooses not to be buried. Let's assume public education is ready to take the first step of many on the road to excellence.

The first step begins with children.

We've only removed the first veil that covers the question, "Who is raising America's children?" The next part of the question to uncover asks something important in three letters.

How?

How?

If parents are sharing their children with a variety of care givers, how are these care givers nurturing their children? Is this another complex, multi-pronged, almost unanswerable question?

Yes.

Will that stop us from trying to answer it?

No.

Let's turn to several internationally respected theorists and thinkers. Sometimes we need to go beyond our own perceptions and emotions and relative smallness in time and space. The day care question is one of these "sometimes." The implications and long-term consequences are just too important to minimize or become clouded by our own personal biases. Day care is no longer a fact just in California and Chicago. Day care exists in every state, city, and town in the United States—it is a growing phenomenon in every nook and cranny of this country. By 1990, there will be almost 24 million preschoolers in the United States. More than half—perhaps closer to two-thirds—will be placed in some type of day care program.[2]

As we turn to several major thinkers, it may be better for us to examine the How? in light of how children grow and develop and, therefore, how we *should* be caring for them.

Turning to the thinkers is something most of us tend to avoid. As a result, our ignorance is showing and our discomfort is acute. Public educators and parents can no longer assume those who plan programs for our children *understand* children and how they grow and develop. Public educators and parents need a brief, plain English interpretation of the thinking of Piaget, Erikson, Bruner, Gesell, and Dreikurs. They can also benefit from a dose of the findings of more contemporary thinkers like Bronfenbrenner, Elkind, and White. Of course there are other researchers who contributed significantly to our knowledge bank but let's begin with these eight. The truth as we see it is this. If all parents and all teachers and all day care workers and care givers understood the *essence* of the work of these eight thinkers, we would be doing a much better job of raising mentally and physically healthy, happy, responsible, cooperative, self-reliant, and self-disciplined children. And the quality of our busy adult lives would increase as a result of a job well-done!

So you don't have time to study the works of these researchers? Sure you do. All you need are a few people to share the sifting of verbiage until bare essence sifts out and remains. Once we reach essence, plain English takes over so understanding can take place. While this book is written as a practical guide to public educators and parents as they wrestle with the day care concept, some significant research findings need examining. This chapter is not the Omega by any means but merely an encourager of future research.

The work of Erik Erikson needs to be understood by anyone who plans programs for children, especially day care children. Erikson is a Harvard psychologist who believes that human beings never stop growing. While his most notable work took place in the 1950s, it has withstood the test of time! The strange part about all of this is that Erikson's research *preceded* the day care movement. His work is seldom, if ever, examined in relation to the day care child and that is a grievous error. Erikson's findings are significant. They apply to *all* children (and adults) but their significance to the child of day care is monumental.

Remember, Erikson's research is on psychosocial development. He never had the child of day care in mind as he constructed his findings in a sequential way. Erikson was simply telling us about *children.* It's up to us to figure out what these findings mean to children who spend many of their waking hours *away* from home and parents.

Erikson believes that each one of us goes through eight major stages in our lifetime. A chart explaining these first four stages follows on page 14. However, before looking at the chart, let's briefly explore Erikson's theories. Erikson's more than fifteen years of research produced a description of the life cycle, including the premise that each cycle of life has a positive *and* a negative component.[3]

One of the key ideas is Erikson's belief that psychosocial development is sequential more than chronological. In other words, by one year of age, a child needs to have the trust/mistrust conflict resolved because the next stage is at hand, ready or not! If trust is not a strong part of the make-up of an 18 month old, the stage of autonomy vs doubt will be difficult. Each new stage builds on the preceding one . . . again, ready or not!

Trust, then, becomes the foundation of our total psycho-

ERIKSON'S PSYCHOSOCIAL DEVELOPMENT THEORY
"FIRST FOUR STAGES OF MAN (WOMAN!)"

Stage	Crisis Conflict		Characteristics		Ego Identity
I Infancy	Trust vs Mistrust	First year of life	Hunger is fed, discomfort is comforted, fears are quieted, needs are met.	Conflict resolved through the acquisition of trust in Mother, in self, and then others.	I trust. I hope!
II Early Childhood	Autonomy vs Doubt	15 months to 4 years	Child challenges parents. Child wants both to "hold on to" and "let go."	Conflict resolved when child senses a balance between rules and freedom and child discovers confidence in self.	I am what I will!
III Play Age	Initiative vs Guilt	4 years to 6 years	Increasing interest in "right and wrong" (thoughts as well as deeds).	Conflict resolved when conscience develops in a healthy way without the burden of guilt.	I am what I will be!
IV School Age	Industry vs Inferiority	6 years to 12 years	The world of school takes precedence. Child sees school failure as a sure sign of worthlessness.	Conflict resolved when school tasks are mastered and child is socially and intellectually accepted.	I am what I learn!

social development. Everything else builds upon it. How well we come out of the trust/mistrust conflict influences how well we'll do with our struggle for self-reliance (autonomy). At this point, it is important to know that Erikson feels a child is never *wholly* successful at resolving each conflict at each developmental stage in a positive way.[4] However, a child needs to emerge more successful than not because the residue, or carryover, can limit a child's ability to succeed in resolving the next major crisis conflict. As Erikson suggests, a shallow or shaky foundation limits the heights and strength of people as well as buildings.

It is difficult to take Erikson's prolific work and condense it on a chart. However, the key elements are not impossible to confine to an 8½ x 11 frame!

Now that the chart is somewhat familiar, the question on everyone's mind must be: What does all this have to do with Day Care?

As we see it, Erikson's research tells us the first two stages of development are already part of a child before he or she enters Kindergarten. Trust and autonomy are either resolved positively or not resolved positively by age four. Hopefully, four-year-olds are more trusting of others and self than *mis*trusting.

What, then, can a day care teacher do to help a child whose behavior says he trusts few people and has little faith in his own ability? Well, just because Erikson says stages are passed through, he doesn't mean the *chance* to acquire trust and autonomy is lost forever. What he means is that if the child hasn't acquired these qualities by Kindergarten entrance, school teachers will, undoubtedly, need to work extra long and hard to help the child strengthen psychosocial development during the length of a school day as well as through the cooperation of parents. The child who comes to school with inadequate nurturing during the preschool years is a child who is heading in the direction of a school career that is riddled with problems and possible failure. The nurturing of trust and self-reliance are critically important for early childhood teachers to consider. Day care staff members are early childhood teachers. Trust must be something to work on each and every day as staff plans the day care "day." Stages I and II must be examined by day care staff through inservice.

Let's go further. When a child enters Kindergarten or first grade, two stages have already passed by and the child is already into Stage III or Play Age. Is it possible that American education, in its quest for knowledge and academic superiority, has neglected to respect a child's NEED for play? Erikson's Stage III implies that children learn and grow BEST through PLAY between the ages of four and six. Yet, play carries a negative connotation in American society and is not perceived as absolutely essential to the mental, social, emotional, and physical well-being of every human being. It *is* absolutely essential.

What this says for us is that play should be the primary curriculum for day care children and Kindergarteners and an important part of curriculum in the primary grades.

Let's now consider Erikson's theory of significant relationships during each early developmental stage.

The most important person to a child during Stage I is the mother. In Stage II, both parents achieve equal importance. Stage III finds the family unit as the most important influence on a child's psychosocial development. Now, as a child is ending his/her Kindergarten experience or beginning first grade, a new stage and crisis resolution is at hand. This Stage IV phase is called Industry vs Inferiority, and teachers, school, and neighborhood become the major influence on the growing child. During all the primary grades, a child is moving through some phase of Stage IV. Erikson tells us that school success is more important at this developmental level than at any other time because children of this age equate the mastery of school tasks with self-worth. School failure or perceived failure during this stage enables inferiority to win out over industry.[5]

Day care and primary teachers need to be aware of their importance to the developing child. There needs to be a conscious effort, then, in building trust, order, acceptance, balance between rules and freedom, and the encouragement of autonomy into every day children are away from home and parents.

If mother is the most important person during a child's first stage of psychosocial development, how does early separation from mother affect the child's Stage I conflict resolution? Will a surrogate mother or day care staff member develop a stronger trust bond with a child than the child–parent bond? Are the weekend hours sufficient for this mother–child bonding to occur so that trust is well-developed during the first year of life? Are day care workers and other care givers able to help children resolve Stage II which encompasses the preschool years? How well-versed are day care employees in regard to a preschooler's need to resolve the "rules and freedom" conflict by age 4?

While Erikson's work is highly respected at the post-graduate level, how many professional educators have bothered to interpret Erikson for the world of day care? Day care programs can be improved simply by incorporating Erikson's findings into daily activities. The first three stages of psychosocial development are critically important to the social, emotional, and intellectual growth of every human being. We do not yet know the long-term effects of day care on a child's psychosocial development. All we can do for now is *sense* effects. If your sensing produces a feeling of uneasiness, you're not alone.

The work of Arnold Gesell, like Erikson's, has withstood the test of time. Gesell Institute publications are well-written, solidly researched and highly readable. The common-sense philosophy of Gesell lives through the work of his heirs. All care givers need exposure to the books written by Ilg, Ames, and other Gesell researchers.

Jerome Bruner is one of the most respected theorists in the world. Since most of his research is written at a high cognitive level, Bruner is not as well-read as he should be! His latest book, however, is written in a highly readable style. Bruner writes about his recent experiences as an observer of preschool children in nursery schools and day care centers. His findings are very interesting. They point out some of the problems related to child care and the quality of preschool programs. Bruner forces us to seriously question what we are doing to and for today's young child. While Bruner's latest book is based on his two-year project in England, all that he writes is significant to the early childhood years in the United States.

One of Bruner's findings is so obvious we tend to ignore it. After observing, systematically, a variety of child care centers and nursery schools, Bruner says, emphatically, that it is impossible to label or define preschool education. There are no two preschool experiences alike. Just saying a child has had "preschool" tells us nothing. This complicates the study of day care because day care is often considered preschool education.[6]

Another point Bruner makes is this. Parents often send little ones to day care or nursery school assuming this will increase their language development and school readiness. A 1980 study finds preschool children are most productive in stretching their social-language capacities when they are in *pairs*. The best social setting for rich "play" is the *pair*, even if the children are engaged in parallel play. The above findings are the result of an extensive study of preschoolers in day care centers and nursery schools. In this study, 9,600 half-minute periods were observed. Only 20 percent of those time periods contain conversations. Bruner asks whether young children are receiving too much social distraction in large groups. He feels that little ones cannot handle a complex social setting. Regarding older preschoolers, Bruner implies it is more stimulating (language-wise) for the child to play with an adult than with another child.[7]

Exploring further the 9,600 half-minute observation periods, while talking *does* occur, it is difficult for connected conversations to take place. When rich conversation did take place, it occurred in places set apart from the main area—little nooks and quiet places, such as under blankets draped over chairs. Rich dialogue seems to require more intimate, quiet settings than most preschools and day care centers provide.

When videotapes of preschool programs in action are compared with videotapes of activities in the home, there is little question about where rich and *connected dialogue* take place—in the home! Bruner surmises that evidence overwhelmingly points out that "the interruptions and good-hearted din of the preschool is surely not ideal, however much it may prepare the child for the rough and tumble of getting a word in edgewise or making oneself heard over the voices of others."

Bruner's evaluation includes the role of management of children in day care centers and nursery schools. He sees the demands upon adults in management alone as leaving little time for rich social conversation! Management duties of preschool teachers and care givers take up most of the adult's time.

Another misconception about "preschool" is that a great deal of time is spent on school readiness activities such as numbers, books, and learning games. Through the 9,600 half-minute observations it was discovered that only 3 percent of the time is spent on school readiness activities. Actually, that's welcome empirical news to those of us who believe "formal" school readiness activities are unnecessary for the vast majority of the "under 5" crowd. It is our opinion that the value of school readiness programs for preschoolers is overrated. Spend a day (or an hour) with a group of preschoolers and discover how much respect they have for formal lessons. Observe and learn about children's capacities and tolerance! Structure within a wholesome framework is a must when planning programs for preschoolers but informal, developmentally appropriate activities need to fill the frame.

The regularity of routine seems to have a stabilizing effect on preschoolers and actually increases the richness of their play. This reinforces our belief that young children desperately need more order in their lives.[8]

Bruner's latest work is something of value. While many parents and day care advocates may find his research disturbing, it is difficult not to take it seriously. Bruner is an intellectual heavyweight and his work merits respect. Bruner expresses concern for the quality of child care. In the United States, almost 60 percent of our mothers of young children work at jobs outside of the home. Child care outside the home is a serious concern.

Probably this century's greatest observer of young children in action is Jean Piaget. It is likely that name-dropping "Piaget" is the national pastime of college professors of education. Yet few of us ever leave college understanding Piaget and being able to apply his findings to real life. The most important research flowing from Piaget's seemingly endless fountain is impossible to determine because everything he offers us is important.

However, for our immediate purpose, let's look at some of the ways Piaget's findings are connected to the child in day care.

Before we look at Piaget's best-known work, *The Stages of Cognitive Development*, let's look at his ideas on thinking and language. Thinking exists before language and will always go beyond the limitations of language. Piaget says children use language three to five years before they actually understand the concepts behind the words. He believes even deaf children, denied language knowledge, grasp these concepts at about the same time as hearing children. Piaget says language is good for general communication but not supremely important to intelligence. Sometimes language can actually get in the way of thinking and become an obstacle to learning.[9]

Piaget sees a need to work on the development of intelligence through perceptual, motor, and visual activities and to put less premium on language during the early years. Learning through the senses builds our thinking foundation.

Too often day care and other preschool curricula emphasize language development and not the development of thinking. This may be one of Piaget's less respected and applied theories. At least curriculum builders do not always respect it. When we rush to attempt to develop language in day care programs, we sometimes neglect the more important area of development: the development of thinking! Thinking is best developed through rich, intimate dialogue between pairs (Bruner) as well as through perceptual motor and visual "play" (Piaget).

And speaking of the development of thinking, Piaget's best-known work needs to be understood and applied in all day care programs and activities.

Piaget identified four major stages or phases of cognitive (thinking) development. Day care workers need to be aware of all four stages which span the first fifteen years of life. The first two, however, must become more than a memorization exercise; they must become second-nature to the day care worker. Day care programs and activities need to be planned with these stages in mind.

Together, let us examine the chart on page 22. The data are gathered from many sources, assimilated, and translated into everyday language.

The works of Dreikurs and White need to reach the hands of educators and care givers. This educator's personal favorite "thinker" is Rudolf Dreikurs. Dreikurs, heir to Adlerian psychology, understands the development of

PIAGET'S *FIRST TWO* STAGES OF COGNITIVE DEVELOPMENT

Stage	Time Span	Characteristics
Sensory-Motor	Birth to 2 years	First three months of life, child learns "accidentally" through reflex action automatic behavior.
		Between three and nine months, child repeats above behavior *voluntarily* and now wants to make things happen. Vision is major coordinator of learning but other senses are partners. Imitation of others appears and emotions emerge. So does actual "play."
Seeing		Between nine and twelve months, child learns to adapt after experimentation. Child can now experience action by *watching*, instead of always needing to learn by *acting* via movement and senses.
Hearing		
Smelling		
Tasting		Between one and two years, curiosity and novelty-seeking behavior develops. Spatial relationships develop upon discovering objects as objects. Objects now become permanent. Sensory-motor learning is slowly giving way to semi-mental functioning. Parallel play exists and is necessary to the developing child. Child believes he is the world—the only one who matters. He is an egocentric learner and needs to be egocentric during this stage.
Touching		
Movement		
Action		
Pre-Operational	2 to 7 years	Between two and four years, language begins repeating and replacing sensory-motor repetition. Child continuously investigates the world as he sees it. Learns through pretending and imaginary play. Play teaches child to assimilate and adapt. "How and Why" are important as child plays. Time is "Now" and that is the only concept of time. A very egocentric stage. Child believes what he sees via appearance, not what is logical to an adult.
Play Speech		
Time		Between four and seven years, child widens his world, accepts others, and becomes less egocentric as a learner. Speech expresses thinking but child can handle only one idea at a time. Parallel play still exists but child increases social participation. True cognition (higher order thinking) begins during this stage. Awareness of relationships emerges and rules of adults are enacted through play. Child continues to learn *best* through play during this entire period.
is		
Now!		
Space		
is		
Here		
The World		
is Me!		

behavioral patterns within the family setting as well as anyone else in his field. His very practical theories are helpful to day care staff as they deal with the daily complexities of misbehavior within a group setting. *Children the Challenge* is a good "starter" book for anyone interested in theories that *work*. Day care staff inservice can include the study of several chapters in *Children the Challenge*.

This writer co-authored a book inspired by the writings of Rudolf Dreikurs. The book, *Misbehavin'*, can be helpful to day care staff as well as teachers of children, Kindergarten through twelfth grade.

Burton White's book, *The First Three Years of Life*, will be helpful to day care workers even though the book is not particularly popular with all day care or Head Start advocates. Yet for more than twenty years, White has been studying young children within the family setting. White, a psychologist and author, reminds us of the critical importance of developmental stages, especially those occurring between eight months and three years. His research cannot be discounted or discredited through emotional heat. White's work is well-documented and deserves serious, open-minded consideration of both parent and day care worker.

One of today's most readable author-educators is David Elkind. While Elkind doesn't necessarily address the child of day care, he nevertheless addresses the child of today and day care children are, of course, children of today. Elkind worries about the disappearance of childhood. He gives us a great deal to reflect upon in his poignant work, "The Hurried Child." What do Elkind's words mean to children whose "social" life begins so early in the day care setting? What do adult themes and out-in-the-open adult activities in the home mean to the psychosocial development of young children? We cannot say for sure. All we can do is watch, listen, and evaluate in a thoughtful, unbiased way.

Cornell psychologist Urie Bronfenbrenner is a leader in

the study of "family" as well as the young child within a group setting. He feels that because of so many single parent families, a large proportion of mothers working outside the home, and children born out of wedlock, the middle class family is beginning to resemble the low-income family of the 1960s. A question–answer format is used effectively in Bronfenbrenner's "The Erosion of the American Family." This article is worth reading because Bronfenbrenner is a thoughtful, rational educator who sees both sides of an issue. His dialogue is excellent and his common sense approach is refreshing. There is no date or publishing reference on the above monograph but Cornell University should be able to successfully direct interested parties.

One of Bronfenbrenner's special strengths is his involvement with Federally funded preschool programs during those turbulent 1960s. Disadvantaged minority children became the target population. They were placed in intervention programs—strikingly similar to present Federally funded day care programs—before they entered formal schooling. Because Federal funds were used, records were *required* and these records now serve as the data for long-term studies. Although data are still being gathered from the programs existing in the '60s, the Department of Health, Education and Welfare published a comprehensive report several years ago entitled "Is Early Intervention Effective?" Bronfenbrenner was among the impressive group of educators compiling these data. Dozens of preschool programs were studied. A great deal of important, useful information grew out of these studies. However, over and over again, a central theme recurs: Parents make the difference in the "education" of preschoolers!

In the four major program categories of the 1960s, long-term gains occurred *only when programs for parents existed concomitantly with programs for preschoolers.* When children received intervention in isolation, apart from parents, gains were either nonexistent or temporary.

Day care programs, therefore, need parent involvement if children and families are to benefit throughout life.

Growing Child: Research Review examines parent involvement in a recent article. The article deals with Dr. Charles Snow's review of sixteen child care studies. No matter what type of child care services are used, parent involvement is the key to quality. Whenever parents are partners, a child care center or "home" is associated with superior care.[10]

The How? of day care is something child advocates are only beginning to assess. It will take years to conclude How? and many more years to decide whether or not it mattered. The easiest How to figure out is How today's parents are *not* establishing families.

This is how they are *not* doing it.

John falls in love with Marsha. No premarital sex beyond heavy breathing. He proposes marriage. She blushingly accepts. A wedding date is set two years in advance. Marsha works in an office and saves most of her paycheck. John finishes college and begins on the bottom rung of the corporate ladder.

By the time the wedding date rolls around, all furniture and household needs have been purchased. There are no bills and no Master Charge debts.

The first baby arrives two years after the wedding. Marsha becomes a full-time mother and John reaches the third rung of the corporate ladder. A second child arrives three years later. Marsha continues full-time motherhood. In addition, she wears an apron, bakes bread, irons John's underwear, joins the Garden Club, and paints the white picket fence every other Summer. John remains on the third rung of the corporate ladder but his salary increases enough to satisfy his career growth needs. He never looks at another woman, even though his secretary is single and looks like Dolly Parton.

John and Marsha and their two perfect children live happily ever after. But now that John and Marsha's family resembles, perhaps, only 15 percent of the families in the United States, for all intents and purposes, John and Marsha are dead.

Or divorced.

Or separated.

Or unmarried but living together.

Or cheating.

Or in therapy.

Or unemployed.

Or holding down four jobs.

Or abusing their children.

Or members of AA.

Or dependent on other chemical "crutches."

Or, otherwise, semi-unhappy.

The perfect family never existed, of course, but we tend to glorify what we believe used to exist. We believe all marriages used to be like John and Marsha's. We long for what used to be . . . or at least for what we *wish* used to be . . . and so we hug our myths.

Of course, we used to be closer to the John and Marsha myth than we are today. Perhaps some of us just wish we could be a little bit closer to the "ideal" of the past.

There are daily signs of a healthy renewal of the family spirit. Parents are gradually reawakening to the crying demand for responsibility in parenthood. We see these signs in our work with hundreds of families and we like what we are seeing.

How we raise our children matters. Dr. Barbara Bowman, director of the Erikson Institute for Advanced Study In Child Development, says, "Early learnings do have a 'sticking quality,' not necessarily for life, but a special quality that tends to underlie later experiences and bias later understandings."

She adds something else to her message. It's all we need to know.

"The experience young children are most vulnerable to is loving parents, that we know for certain.[11]"

What Does All of This Mean to Children?

Kerry is wakened each weekday at 5:30 A.M. His mother lifts her two-year-old sleepyhead from his warm crib, wraps a blanket around him, and carries him to the car. She drives Kerry to his day care center ten miles away. Then she backtracks ten miles, passes her house, and continues another two miles to work. Twenty-two miles traveled twice a day are paying their toll on Kerry's mother, her car, and possibly Kerry himself. We cannot know for sure. We can only guess.

We also cannot know for sure how much "mothering" Kerry's mom can physically and emotionally offer Monday through Friday. She picks up Kerry at the day care center about 4:30 P.M., drives home, heats dinner, and tends to the washing, cleaning, and assorted daily inevitables of life.

Kerry sees his daddy on Saturdays. On Sundays he sees his paternal grandparents in the morning and his maternal grandparents in the afternoon. Sunday nights are spent at home with Mom, watching television.

Monday morning at 5:30 A.M., Kerry is lifted from his crib and the cycle begins once more.

What does Erikson's work tell us about Kerry? He has passed from Stage I to Stage II. Has he acquired trust in himself and others? With whom did he spend the waking hours of that first critical year of life? How are his day care center teachers and aides helping him acquire the necessary balance between rules and freedom and the "holding onto and letting go" conflict?[12]

Between the ages of two and four the child's striving for mastery or control is strong. He wants, on one hand, to be a baby and depend on parents and, on the other hand, he wants independence and the capacity for self-help and control. The mother, especially, is in conflict with the child at this time because of her need to "hold onto" as well as "let go." And so both mother *and* child are experiencing similar emotions and behavior during this stage of a *child's* development.[13]

And what does Piaget's work tell us about Kerry's development of thinking? A two-year-old is more an infant than a preschooler and still needs a great deal of sensory-motor activity. Do Kerry's day care teachers and aides understand this sensory-motor period of development? Do they understand that Kerry is preparing to enter the stage called "Preoperational" and that "play" is the key to learning between the ages of two and seven? Do they understand the meaning and importance of parallel play and that sharing and taking turns are not yet ready to emerge and can't be expected? Do they understand what egocentric means and that it is a *necessary* part of a young child's makeup, like it or not?

Dreikurs would tell us Kerry's behavioral patterns are being influenced by *all* the adults and children with whom he interacts. While patterns of behavior were historically developed during the first five years of life within the confines of *family*, what does Kerry's day care and fragmented family experiences mean to the development of the way he moves through life, behaviorally? Does it matter—will it matter— that Kerry spends about fifty hours a week with as many as six different day care employees and twenty-seven other preschoolers? Does it matter—will it matter—that Kerry spends Saturdays only with his daddy and Sunday split-shifts with two sets of different-point-of-view grandparents?

Does it matter—will it matter—that Kerry spends only ten to fifteen waking hours a week with his mother? Despite the quality of those ten to fifteen hours, is that enough time for critical mother–child bonding to occur? What does Burton White tell us about the mother–child relationship during those first three years of life?

Put yourself in Kerry's place. See yourself as a two-year-old, lying in a warm crib, lost in Never-Never-Land. Sense someone (no matter how gently) lifting you from your warmth and comfort and carrying you, half-asleep, to a waiting car. Sit or half-lie on the car seat among today's jeans, underwear, T-shirt, socks, sneakers, and lunchbag. Miss your Paddington Bear and begin to cry for it. Be told to stop crying. Ask to go back in the house to get Paddington. Be told you can't because that would make Mommie late for work. Cry again. Get scolded again. Say you're hungry. Be told, gently, that you have to wait until you get to the center. Fall asleep the final eight miles. Sense someone (no matter how gently) lifting you from your warmth and comfort and carrying you, half-asleep, to a waiting day care teacher.

It is now 5:50 A.M. Your long, long day is twenty minutes old. Say "goodbye" to Mommie and join more than a dozen other pajama-clad kids for O.J. and cereal.

Be honest. How does it feel to be Kerry? How did you like putting yourself in his place?

Kerry's mother loves him and spends as much quality time with him as she possibly can. How do you think it feels to be Kerry's mother? How would you like to put yourself in her place?

Tricia's mother's boyfriend is unemployed so Tricia spends three days at home with him and two days at day care. Bobby (mother's boyfriend) is eighteen years old. Tricia is three. In many ways, Tricia is more mature than Bobby. She gets breakfast for herself and Bobby. Then they watch TV all morning. Bobby drinks beer for lunch. Tricia knows that beer and Bobby don't mix well. By the time Bobby finishes his second can, Tricia stays as far away from him as she can. She finds little hiding places in the small apartment until she hears Bobby snoring. Then she tip-toes out and sits by the window, watching for Mommie to come home. She watches for two hours. When she sees the car turn the corner a block away, she runs to the kitchen to get a snack out of the refrigerator for herself and Mommie. Then she rushes back to the window to wait just a little longer.

Tricia isn't sure whether she likes Mondays, Wednesdays, and Fridays better than Tuesdays and Thursdays. It's hard for her to figure out if the day care center is more fun than being home three days with Bobby. How does Tricia's "thinking" relate to Piaget's findings? How does Tricia's psychosocial development relate to Erikson's work? What would Dreikurs tell us about the way Tricia's patterns of behavior are forming?

Kerry and Tricia are real children. They are typical or nearly typical of the 12 million or more preschoolers receiving daytime care from adults other than parents. Actually, Kerry and Tricia are two of the more fortunate children. While their daily lives are disruptive and confusing, they *are* loved and wanted by at least one parent. We aren't going to visit the unloved, unwanted, and abused preschoolers through this book. Just knowing they exist in the millions is motivating enough to feel constructive, active anger welling inside. Public educators, awaken!

Saying Kerry's mother should stay home and raise her own child is a fantasy solution. Saying Tricia's mom should get rid of her teenage boyfriend is a waste of words. The fact is this: Kerry and Tricia are dependent upon their parent's decision-making. Kerry and Tricia, as preschoolers, have no choice in the matter. While children are decision-makers, they are not adult situation-makers. Children's decisions are things such as "Do I want a cheese or bologna sandwich?"

"Do I want to cry or do I want to put a bandage on my knee?" Children's decisions do *not* include, "Do I want to live with Mommie and Daddy or Mommie and Bobbie or just Mommie?" "Do I want to be taken from my warm bed at 5:30 A.M. or do I want to sleep longer?"

The decision-making and situation-making of parents *has to* have some effect on the way children grow up. Is the effect positive or negative? Is the effect measurable in degrees of plus and minus? Is adult situation-making a measurable influence on children?

When Kerry is fifteen years old, will it matter that he rode in the car a hundred miles a week to and from day care or that his mother was exhausted most of the time? When Tricia is fifteen years old, will it matter that she spent so much time watching TV with Bobby in the morning and hiding from him in the afternoon?

Who can say? There are no answers, only more questions.

We say children are this country's most precious natural resource. Yet *collectively*, we do not follow our words with caring action. We are good at falling in love with *one* child but not with *all* children.

Consider the thoughts of Ellen Goodman as she expands upon this premise. Very eloquently, Goodman weaves the wonderment of Elizabeth Jordan Carr's test-tube conception. Then she weaves a connecting idea.

> She is in some ways the creature of a system which responds well to private needs, is engaged dramatically in producing happy endings to personal stories. We do better for individuals than for masses. We give more applause to the extraordinary than to the mundane.
>
> Tell us about an abandoned baby and we will call by the hundreds with offers of food, money, even adoption. Tell us about a child who will not survive without a fancy operation and we will set up a fund to buy its health.
>
> But tell us about the 40,000 children who die every day in the world and our eyes glaze over at impersonal numbers. Tell us that 13 out of a thousand infants will die in this coun-

try and it seems remote. Talk about nutrition for two million of the poor and pregnant and we do not find it . . . urgent.

Perhaps, after all, we need a glossy magazine photo of each pregnant woman who promises to send baby pictures if we keep her in flour and cheese and milk.

After watching Elizabeth's performance, I went back to the Natural History magazine on my lap. I read an article about birds that only feed their offspring if they stay within the nesting circle. If one goes a foot beyond the invisible marker, the parents will ignore the cries of their own young.

Society's a bit like that, I thought. We care for those who live within a certain circumference, or who capture our attention because they are extraordinary. We let some in and keep others out. And we don't ask ourselves often enough to expand the circle of caring.[14]

And if children are this country's most precious natural resource, why do only three states require an early childhood degree for day care teachers? Is that the way we expand our caring circle? While academic degrees do not guarantee quality, a degree in early childhood at least *suggests* quality and fitness and readiness to work with young children. The National Day Care Study (Ruopp et al, 1979) suggests "small groups, supervised by lead caregivers with *career* preparation in child development and early childhood" are essential for quality child care. The study further suggests that the philosophy of the staff and the implementation of that philosophy in curriculum or program are critical to quality. People make the program and qualified people make quality programs. All of this is common sense. And yet an examination of day care licensing requirements reveals that requirements vary a great deal from state to state. Even the adult–child ratio requirement fluctuates between 20:1 and 5:1.

Nevada is the only state with the admirable ratio of 5:1. Mississippi is the only state that has no adult–child ratio requirements. (Mississippi, what do you have to say for yourself?)

Of course, the findings of a 1979 study will have been more accurate in 1979. Changes have undoubtedly been made. Ironically, *some* changes were not for the better! The author of the article to which we refer summarizes his thoughts this way:

> This review of state child care regulations reveals little change from the 1978 to 1982 reports: It would appear that states have paid little heed to the child care research. Neither the findings that point toward improved child outcomes nor those that highlight favorable cost-quality tradeoffs have been acted upon by most states. Perhaps not enough time has passed.[15]

Perhaps not. Perhaps this country hasn't been scared and sickened enough by the consequences of poor child care during the early years.

It is truly a miracle that so many loving and lovable adults continue to be drawn into the day care circle of employment. If our words and the feelings behind those words in any way suggest that most day care workers are lacking skills, dedication, and warmth, apologies are in order. The miracle to which we allude in the preceding sentence is the fact that so many warm, dedicated, skilled adults are willing to work so intensively for so little monetary compensation. *Many* day care employees continue to earn subminimum wages while the majority receive minimum or a shade above minimum without much hope of future increase.

The following was taken from the text of a speech given at the NAEYC 1982 conference by Georgianna Roberts. She charges child care leaders with several tasks:

> Our first task will be to inform all workers about the harsh realities of jobs in the child care field. Most are unaware of child caregivers' shockingly low wages and low status which cause dissatisfaction and attrition. Many child caregivers are paid less than the minimum wage, work an exhausting eight to ten hours a day, have no substitutes or paid vacations, and

no job security or health or retirement benefits. Clearly, child care needs and deserves more economic and social support to carry out its important task.[16]

If our task is to nurture children in the ways they need nurturing and *if* parents are going to continue working outside the home and *if* parents place their children in child care centers or homes and *if* child care employees continue to be grossly, embarrassingly underpaid, what does this mean to children?

Qualified and high-quality day care staff tend to leave child care employment as soon as a higher-paying job comes along. Most day care teachers and aides in our area of the country tell us the turnover of staff is alarming. They express their genuine concern for the children. As soon as the children become attached to an adult, that adult leaves and another comes to take her place. One day care director told us she loses a staff member every three months because of her inability to pay higher wages. This director said, "You lose the best ones. It's a crying shame but I can't stay afloat if I pay the aides more than minimum wage and the teacher more than $4 an hour."

Until adults with power and influence begin seeing what happens when our children and their "nurturers" are placed on the low priority shelf, the quality of child care will be ignored. Of course, quality will not be ignored by child advocates. Unfortunately child advocates usually lack the political clout necessary for essential change in the day care movement.

Essential change in day care includes higher wages for caregivers as well as improved working conditions and benefits.

While child advocates intensify their persuasive message to powerful political figures, let us examine the significance of "attachment." It is connected to the high staff turnover in the world of day care.

The term attachment is, perhaps, the most emotional one facing the entire day care movement. One of the purposes of this book is to look at all studies and thinking, no matter how emotionally laden.

While the early work of Rene Spitz has not completely held up, at least his ideas opened up a whole new area of study: the first year of life, specifically attachment to one figure.[17]

Perhaps we can refer to John Bowlby as the father of attachment. His research in this area is impressive and worthy of mention. Bowlby's books (or key chapters) need to be read by mothers, fathers, teachers, day care directors, and other caregivers. Bowlby himself is unpopular with some advocates of the day care movement. Bowlby's research does not always tell day care advocates what they want to hear. Bowlby's findings make sense to us, however. We tend to gravitate toward Bowlby's light because we believe early separation of child and mother disturbs the fibers of attachment.

Among other things, Bowlby asks four powerful questions. These questions are relevant to the theme of day care, even though the day care movement had hardly begun when Bowlby immersed himself in attachment research.

Bowlby asks:

(a) Do children commonly direct their attachment behavior towards more than one person?
(b) If they do so, do attachments to a number of figures develop simultaneously or does one attachment always precede the others?
(c) When a child has more than one figure to whom he is attached, does he treat all figures alike or does he show a preference for one of them?
(d) Can a woman other than a child's natural mother fill adequately the role of principal attachment-figure?[18]

Elsewhere, Bowlby suggests that attachment to mother or the major caregiver does not occur, miraculously, between six and nine months of age. Instead, it develops from about the third or fourth month although observable attachment *behavior* doesn't emerge until the sixth or seventh month.

The first few weeks of life, *readiness* to develop attachment is relatively low. It heightens during the fourth, fifth, and sixth months and then becomes *observable*.[19]

In still another portion of Bowlby's studies, he writes,

> No form of behavior is accompanied by stronger feeling than is attachment behavior. The figures toward whom it is directed are loved and their advent is greeted with joy. So long as a child is in the unchallenged presence of a principal attachment-figure, or within easy reach, he feels secure. A threat of loss creates anxiety, and actual loss sorrow, both, moreover, and likely to arouse anger.[20]

More than any other area of child development, attachment to parents, especially mother, seems to be the foundation for the quality of life! How well we attach to our major caregiver determines how well we fare in all future relationships. Who is our child's major caregiver? Does it matter if he or she is not mother? Are we messing around with the natural flow of things when we separate child from parent too early?

All our research—and it goes way beyond the studies shared in this book—suggests that, yes, we are getting in the way of Mother Nature but it may be ten or twenty more years before we can measure the consequences.

Can we afford to wait ten or twenty years?

Can the children wait?

In the meantime, the attachment or bonding that takes place between the child of day care and the day care employee *must* be healthy, strong, trusting, and loving. We must "imitate" Mother Nature as best we can!

However, let us never forget that we are imitating the real

thing and not replacing it with a superior way of living and growing.

Let us never forget that.

We've briefly touched upon the significance of the work of Erikson, Piaget, Bruner, Gesell, Dreikurs, White, Bronfenbrenner, and Elkind. We're still wrestling with the question we're asking in this chapter: What does the world of day care mean to children? After less than a year of establishing and operation a day care center for our district's preschoolers, we in the Wilson District ask that question every day.

Our day care center's program has to respect the tenets of the great thinkers and then apply them. It does.

Developing trust in self and others (Erikson) is a daily unspoken theme. Learning through movement and the senses, understanding parallel play, emphasizing the development of *thinking* before emphasizing the development of language and respecting the essence of play (Piaget) are woven into daily plans. "Grouping" children more carefully and being conscious of the importance of the "pair" in play and the creation of intimate "nooks and crannies" are considered in the physical set-up of the center (Bruner).

And on and on and on. . . .

We are so seriously concerned about the well-being—the foreverness—of our day care children, we most likely overevaluate our program. While we are feeling better than good about our home-away-from-home, we continue to feel uneasy about the day care movement itself. There is something unnatural about placing preschoolers in a room filled with other young children on a daily basis. Even our home-away-from-home atmosphere is a fabricated mood. We can't replicate "home." We know that. Of course, we continue to try. We'd be more concerned if our day care center resembled an institution or a sterile, uninviting cavern, which it doesn't.

There is also something unnatural about a 10:1 child–adult ratio. As Bruner explains, the best ratio during the preschool years is 1:1. The richest dialogue takes place in the home between parent and child. Our day care center never violates Pennsylvania's 10:1 ratio requirement. Much of the time we enjoy 6:1.

But even one adult for every six children might not be good enough for the total well-being of the developing child.

We believe Bronfenbrenner's assessment of parent involvement in preschool programs and make sure our parents feel *totally* involved. We encourage our parents to "hang around" for awhile before and/or after their day care needs are met. Our parents are invited to play for a little while with their children before leaving the center. Written communications flourish and we find it impossible to over-communicate.

Still, is what we are doing "right" for young children?

No.

Then is it second-best?

Probably not. Second-best is most likely a loving grandma or aunt. At a conference a few years ago at Kutztown University, Burton White told his audience that a blood-relative is probably second-best to mother as caregiver. White said a preschooler *must* spend her waking hours with someone who is crazy about her. He said adult caregivers are more likely to fall in love with children to whom they "belong," like grandchildren, nieces, or nephews.

If we're not doing second-best, we'd better be third-best. Are we?

Yes. We are.

Is third-best good enough?

We are good *for* and *with* the children in our care. We believe our day care program is excellent. We believe there's none better than ours. But we don't pretend to be as good for preschoolers as are caring parents or grandparents in a loving home.

And when we become overly concerned about our involvement with—and now our commitment to—day care, we remind ourselves of the alternatives. We remind ourselves that the places some of the children could be are fourth-best, fifth-best, sixth-best, seventh-best, etc. and then we are glad the children are with us.

Third-best suddenly looks a lot better for the little ones. Our home-away-from-home is a healthy, safe, happy place for all the children who spend their day with us.

We've come a long way from our months and years of studying the *idea* of establishing a district-operated day care center. Now we'd like to help other public schools explore this idea. Perhaps we can smooth the way somewhat. Maybe we can even help others avoid some of the lumps and bumps we experienced as we broke with tradition.

We hope so.

We've devoted the next ten chapters to helping other school districts attempt what we made happen.

The following chapters represent our "How to. . . ."

We want others to learn "How to . . . " for many reasons. One reason belongs to Erikson. As he tells us, a young child learns whether the world is a good, trusting, happy, orderly place in which to be or a powerful, frustrating, miserable, uncertain place. He learns these things early because he needs to know. You see, he is dependent on the outside world for a long time.[21]

Nobody's Listening

Nobody is listening.

The year is 1979. Public school Kindergarten enrollment continues to decline. I explore behind the scenes to find out where all the children have gone. I discover, via census and district data, that they are in Aunt Hildy's Progressive Kindergarten-Day Care or Mr. Pringle's Funtime Kindergarten or any number of private all-day Kindergartens operating in our county. Some of these private day care centers enjoy good reputations. Unfortunately, many do not. Are parents aware of the consequences of placing their young child in unwholesome child care homes or centers?

Even though I am concerned about the loss of students, I am bothered less by declining enrollment than I am by a disturbing pattern our first grade teachers are discovering. Many of the children entering first grade who did *not* go through our district's Kindergarten program are experiencing difficulties, behaviorally and academically. We notice this pattern continuing after the first few weeks and months of school—and on into second and third grades. Teachers in other districts tell me the same thing. We need to study this pattern.

I begin asking myself the question nobody wants to hear. Why can't public school districts establish day care centers

40

for Kindergarten children? Why can't public schools reach out to little ones before their developmental jello sets? Can we make a difference? Can public administrators and Boards of Education read the handwriting on the wall? Can they "connect" the relationship between meeting children's varied needs in a quality way and declining enrollment? Will they decide to reshape the frame of public education to include emphasis on early childhood? Will they recognize that their very future depends on looking at young children through different eyes—eyes that see public schools as care-givers *before* a child is officially age-eligible for school?

I begin asking my fellow educators the questions they don't want me to ask. They refuse to listen.

Nobody is listening.

I am not good at being ignored—especially when children and education are concerned—especially when the home–school bond can be strengthened by addressing these questions.

I am stubborn. I create a plan in my head, transfer it to paper, and present it to educational leaders. I ask if they will read my plan for the children—for us—and give it serious consideration. I ask them to take a few months to consider these ideas before coming to a conclusion. I even hit them in another area. If we open a day care center, we might be able to save the closing of another elementary school. If we open a day care center, we will be able to employ more teachers. If we open a day care center, we will be able to give public education much-deserved recognition. The public is ready for change. Public educators need to be ready, too.

Six months pass.

A year passes.

Eighteen months pass.

No response.

Someone in a neighboring school district shows interest in this Kindergarten Day Care plan. He begins listening.

Within a year, a comprehensive early childhood program

is firmly established. It is educationally sound but does not yet include day care. A second year passes. The last major component of our early childhood program is just about ready to enter the world of public education. The idea whose time has come has arrived at last.

Wilson District's Kindergarten Day Care Program is ready for birth—the first of its kind in the state of Pennsylvania.

August 29, 1983.

Twenty-three Kindergarteners.

Four staff members.

All ours.

Public education is getting a boost forward but it doesn't know it yet. We blaze a trail for others to follow. Anybody can do it—and do it well. All you have to do is care about to-day's child, today's parent, today's teacher, and today's school . . . and tomorrow's quality of life.

If you are a public (or private) educator and you care enough, you'll be able to follow our plan of action. You, too, will be able to establish and operate a Kindergarten Day Care Center in one of your schools.

And you'll be able to do it without using local taxpayer money, Title XX funds, or other Federal or State assistance.

You'll be running on your own steam and feeling darned good about your independence.

Quality day care in public school without the use of Federal funds?

You betcha!

This is how we did it.

Before exploring ideas with Board members and the community-at-large, we need to agree on a philosophy. Our district's Superintendent, Assistant Superintendent, and Elementary Principals never have a problem agreeing on philosophy. Here is what we believe: Every child is precious. Every child needs to feel safe, confident, and wanted. Every child deserves a child care program that respects the laws of growth and provides for individual needs and abilities. Every child deserves a program that is developmentally appropriate.

We also believe preschoolers need a great deal more one-on-one adult–child interaction than most day care centers can provide. While we believe that *most* day care center employees are caring, dedicated, hard-working individuals, we also believe *most* day care center employees are under-paid, overworked, and underappreciated! For many, many reasons, child care has a low priority for those who have the power to upgrade child care priority in this country.

Day care employees, therefore, do not enjoy the respect and status they deserve. As a result, day care staff turnover is very, very high. Children suffer when their relationships with trusted, caring adults get severed with alarming fre-quency. Children suffer when they are in a constant state of emotional adjustment. The powers-to-be need a good "educating!" Only they can do something about this frightening phenomenon in a global sense.

We believe the adult–child ratio is too high in most centers. Family day care offers a smaller adult–child ratio and research suggests the fewer children per adult, the bet-ter for each child's development. Our day care center, there-fore, needs to combine the best qualities of home-care with the best qualities of center-based care.

Our center will become a home-away-from-home. We will accept nothing less for our little ones.

The activation of our day care philosophy can help only a few. We can and will do something about the situation within our district but we don't have the clout to go beyond.

And we need to go beyond.

Perhaps this handbook will help.

After articulating philosophy, we needed to explore two questions and decide on one direction. Do we want to tie in with our local Intermediate Unit's Preschool Program or do we want to establish and operate an independent Wilson District day care program?

Deciding on the latter had absolutely nothing to do with the quality of the Intermediate Unit 14 preschool program. We visited I.U. operated centers and we met several times with the Director of Preschool Programs. The Director is dynamic and first rate! She oversees all Intermediate Unit operated day care services and she pursues quality. Our decision not to establish a partnership with the I.U. was based on a simple educational dream, a concept unanimously supported by Administrators and Board of Education members.

Let's do it ourselves. Let's take care of our district's children. Let's employ Wilson residents. Let's create a home-away-from-home. Let's create a high quality, low cost program so parents won't need to seek Federal funds. Let's encourage parents to pay their own way—to meet responsibility by reaching into their own wallets.

Let's do it ourselves because, suddenly, *everybody's* listening.

Planting The Day Care Seed

Any farmer worth her bib overalls knows the ground needs to be "made ready" for planting. Sowing seeds in unprepared or rocky soil is foolish, especially when the future harvest is already promised to children.

Step 1 in establishing a day care center in a public school has to be:

> DO YOUR HOMEWORK

What kind of homework?

Research and reading, visiting established day care centers (some will welcome you, others will not), interviewing day care directors, day care supervisors, day care aides and day care parents, observing preschoolers in different kinds of environments.

Doing your homework is time-consuming so be careful not to rush through it. Data gathering and conceptualizing are critically important and will demand a time-frame of between six months to a year.

I will admit to having spent more than three years doing my day care homework. Perhaps I am slow at conceptualizing. Perhaps I am overly cautious. Whatever the reasons, I feel I *needed* that amount of time to prepare myself and others for innovation.

After I felt comfortable with my homework phase of the day care journey, I began compiling my data in a sequence that would make sense to others. My data gathering covered a historical period of almost forty years. I now understood the evolution of the day care movement. I now understood that men who blame today's women for the day care movement are pointing their index finger in the wrong direction. Probably the first day care center established in the U.S. was at the Kaiser Shipbuilding Corp. during World War II. It seems that when men go off to war, someone has to mind the factories. And when that "someone" is Mom, someone *else* must mind the kids!

After World War II ended, some "Moms" didn't rush back to the exclusivity of the kitchen. And so, very slowly, the day care movement crept forward. With each passing year of creeping, the complexity increased. Today, the whole day care issue is a maze of complication and crisis.

Being able to put things in sequence and being able to explain this complexity in simple ways is an indication that your initial homework phase is completed. At this point you should be armed with:

A. A brief history of day care in the U.S.
B. Articles from educational publications, popular magazines, local newspapers, the *Wall Street Journal*, and other respected newspapers.
C. Quotes and phrases gathered from your interviews with day care workers and parents.
D. Information on the developmental needs of preschool age children.
E. Enrollment statistics from your own district including how many children are *eligible* for Kindergarten and how many are actually enrolled.

Let's expand on item "E."

The difference between those enrolled and those eligible may surprise you. If you are losing 10 percent or more to private schools, you may want to assess the all around *quality* of education in your district. Remember, your goal is *not* to put private schools out of business. Your goal is to provide quality education for those children who *choose* to attend public school.

Establishing a day care program in a poor quality public school is a bad idea. Establishing a day care center in a *good* public school is what we're after. No advertising is necessary when you do what's right for children.

Watch what happens to your enrollment when you improve the quality of your Kindergarten and first grade programs at the same time you establish a day care center. It's amazing.

Of course, if you are already enrolling most of your community's eligible-for-Kindergarten children, then don't look for the impossible. However, establishing a day care center need not be based upon declining enrollment. Establishing day care services should first and foremost be a symbol of caring about today's child in today's changing family. When there is a connection between day care and school, there is a natural cementing of the home–school bond.

F. A simple outline, proposal, or plan of action including projected income and expenses.

Hopefully, you will have met several times with the Superintendent and/or other administrators during this homework phase.

When you feel comfortable with your rationale and your proposal, it is time to address the Board of Education. Ask the Superintendent (unless you *are* the Superintendent) to invite you to the next Board meeting. Encourage *all* Board members to attend the meeting so your presentation is heard by everyone.

If you are hoping to begin operating a day care center in September of 1986, make your Board presentation by November of 1985! Give yourself all the time you can. You'll need it.

You are now at Step 2:

MAKE A PRESENTATION TO THE BOARD OF EDUCATION

When addressing the Board, be prepared to convince the members to give you permission to *explore* the day care idea with the community. You are neither seeking nor demanding Board *approval* for establishing a day care center. You are merely *looking into* the day care needs of the community.

Speak to the Board briefly and enthusiastically or stay home. If you don't believe in what you're proposing, neither will they. Do not give them anything to read while you are speaking. Address those six areas that grew out of your homework phase. *After* verbally exploring these areas, give each Board member a written outline or tentative proposal. Do not go beyond one sheet of paper, although you'll probably offer data on both sides of that single sheet.

Hopefully, by the end of your presentation, the Board will agree to your sending a questionnaire to parents. If the Board wants more thinking time, do not feel discouraged. Smile and tell them you're glad you work for a district that doesn't rush new ideas. Luckily, my Board members voted 9–0 that same evening and the next morning I prepared a questionnaire.

Step 3, then is:

> PREPARE A SIMPLE QUESTIONNAIRE FOR PARENTS
> AND DECIDE HOW TO DISTRIBUTE IT

Our questionnaire is in the appendix.
Step 4 quickly follows Step 3:

> ASSESS DAY CARE QUESTIONNAIRES AND DECIDE
> IF A DAY CARE CENTER IS NEEDED AND WANTED

You'll need to receive 50 percent more requests for day care than you'll actually be able to accommodate. You'll discover why in a later chapter.

Step 5:

> ASK BOARD TO APPROVE YOUR DAY CARE CENTER
> *PROPOSAL* AS A ONE-YEAR PILOT PROGRAM

Of course, if there is not sufficient interest, this is THE END, at least for the present!

In order to help you in preparing a common-sense report to the Board, I'm sharing the essence of my message to our Board on November 17, 1982.

"My personal wish for *all* children is that they get to grow up in a warm, loving family where Mom and Dad love each other as well as their children and one parent works outside the home and the other parent does not work outside the home full-time until the youngest child begins school. Unfortunately, my personal wish will come true for perhaps 20 percent of this nation's children. If current trends continue, this 20 percent estimate will be wiped away.

"In only 10 years, the number of single parent families doubled—from 3.3 million to 6.6 million! Of these 6.6 million families, almost 3 million are headed by a divorced woman.

"More than half of the preschoolers in the U.S. have mothers who work outside the home.

"I could go on and on, citing one statistic after another but let's not. The picture is very clear. It is probably a picture none of us likes. What is happening to families and children and society-in-general probably goes against our value system. All around us, sacred ideas seem to be crumbling. It's scary.

"But we can't *be* scared and we can't run away from life and we can't moralize and we can't stop an unstoppable force.

"I can do nothing about 6.6 million single parent families. I can do nothing about the high divorce rate, the epidemic levels of child abuse, 50 percent of mothers of young children working outside the home. All I can do is accept that all these changes are occurring—like it or not—and then figure out how we can help others cope with change and become happier, mentally healthier people.

"I've come to several conclusions over the years. One of the best conclusions I've reached is this: I use up as much energy *opposing* an unstoppable force as I do when I harness the force and guide it in a better direction. That's how it is for all of us in the field of education.

"Day Care is one of those things I opposed vehemently until a few years ago when I realized my energy was being wasted on something that could not be stopped. That's when I became more open-minded to the issue and started studying it with more objectivity. After lots of research, I came to see the value in establishing day care centers in public schools. I assure you it has taken me a long time to reach this point. I study things very carefully because decisions made for young children deserve only our best efforts.

"Tonight I'd like you to think about one of those conclusions I reached after lots of agonizing. I'd like you to consider the Day Care concept as Wilson's contribution to *bettering* the unstoppable force.

"Let's create our own Day Care Center.

"Let's make it a happy home-away-from-home."

The day care proposal was approved unanimously. It was a miracle kind of event and I felt very, very proud of these overseers of the Wilson District. They couldn't fully perceive it then, but their decision was to become monumental.

Step 6:

> INFORM THE BOARD ON A MONTHLY BASIS

Assure the Board members that you will keep them fully informed on a monthly basis through the Superintendent or other administrator.

The seed planting is completed. Now the REAL work begins.

Hoe, Hoe, Hoe

Now that you have a plan of action, what do you do with it?

Well you will discover that you will be doing an awful lot of hoeing over the next few months.

You will also discover how many critically important details escaped you during seed planting.

By the time this period of hoeing ends, your original proposal will have been altered twenty or thirty times.

I kid you not.

Let's look at this stage in the development of Wilson's day care program. We took six major steps between June, 1981 and November, 1982. Once we received Board approval on November 17, 1982, we had to consider the following questions:

(1) Should we operate a center for four- and five-year-olds or should we operate only a Kindergarten day care center?
(2) Which building should house our center?
(3) Since our district operates seven elementary buildings, how will we transport children from those buildings to our day care center?
(4) How will we ever meet several hundred Department of

Welfare regulations? (Day Care centers must be licensed by the Department of Welfare. Centers must also receive a certificate of Occupancy from the Department of Labor and Industry.)

(5) When should we advertise for staff? (We figured we would need to hire four staff members for a 20-children center.)

(6) Will our projected income meet our projected expenses? (This is the scariest question since taxpayer money or Federal funds would not be used.)

Obviously, other questions arose during this phase of readiness but these were the most important ones.

This is how we answered each question:

(1) We decided to operate a center for Kindergarten children only. There appeared to be enough Kindergarten parents interested in order to "carry" the financial operation. Another reason for this decision is that we could shut down the center while the children were in Kindergarten classes across the hall. This shut-down would reduce our payroll and we needed to watch out for every dollar we spent.

(2) Our first choice was a Jr. High building. We liked this idea because it would give secondary students a chance to interact with the day care children. In addition, the Jr. High building is located next to our largest elementary school. The children could walk to Kindergarten class and then return to day care after school.

Eventually we decided to create our day care center in the largest elementary school—the Whitfield building. It would be better during inclement weather to have the children's day care room located across the hall from Kindergarten. So that we could involve secondary students in our day care program, tentative plans were outlined with the help of one of our Sr. High home-economics teachers.

(3) The question of transportation became a minor concern because most of the day care children would be driven by parents to and from the day care center between the hours of 6:30 A.M. and 5:30 P.M. However, several of the day care children could board a bus at their neighborhood school and be transported to the Whitfield School as long as we didn't have to provide special transportation. If day care children could hitch a ride on a regular bus run, fine. When a district's Superintendent, Assistant Superintendent, and Board members are committed to the day care idea, major transportation problems simply dissipate.

(4) Meeting 261 Department of Welfare regulations seemed impossible. However, by August 9 (3 weeks before we opened our center), we easily met 259 and wrote waivers for the remaining two (Regulation 125: Screens at the windows and Regulation 129: A telephone and separate listing). Both areas of non-compliance were justified, in writing, and our compromise plans were eventually approved.

Since our center was to be housed in a public school, we easily met the requirements of the Department of Labor and Industry.

(5) We decided to advertise four day care positions in March. The Elementary Principals would handle initial interviews and the Superintendent and I would interview the final candidates early in May.

(6) Experimenting with a variety of payment plans suggested that we could operate a center that would pay its own way. Our center would be a break-even, non-profit enterprise. We decided to charge parents a dollar an hour plus a dollar a day to cover lunch and snack costs. The time the children spent in Kindergarten would, of course, be free of charge. We agreed that no parent would pay more than $40 a week, including lunch costs. Two parents would pay as little as $10 a week. Average

weekly costs would be $25. This is our "April" break-
down of income. Let us refer to each parent as "Smith"
in order to protect confidentiality.

Smith #1	$ 35
Smith #2	35
Smith #3	40
Smith #4	10
Smith #5	20
Smith #6	23
Smith #7	35
Smith #8	17
Smith #9	40
Smith #10	40
Smith #11	37
Smith #12	20
Smith #13	15
Smith #14	33
Smith #15	14
Smith #16	15
Smith #17	10
Smith #18	35
Smith #19	40
Total weekly income	$514

And so the hoeing part of our day care project was near-
ing an end. It was April, 1983. Our day care center was
scheduled to open its doors on August 29. The period between April and August became our nurturing stage. There
were lots of new growth to handle with loving and caring
hands . . . and infinite frustration.

In order to help you get through the hoeing phase, we're
including in the Appendix a number of forms and communications. They saw us through another stage of development
and they might be useful to you, as well.

And now—on to nurturing.

On second thought, forget nurturing for the moment. There's too much weeding and worrying to do.

Weeding, Worrying

This was, by far, the most difficult phase of our day care project.

So near and yet so far.

Sometimes so far from the grasp of reality I wanted to quit. I wanted to admit defeat in June and July. I wanted us to throw in the towel by August 1.

In retrospect, I believe my feelings went beyond sheer terror at the thought of day care actually becoming a fact. Then again, an innovative goal is more exciting during the anticipatory stage than it is during the reality stage. While I believe this common mood-change was part of my feelings as we closed in on D-Day, I consider it a minor influence. Finally I attributed my wanting to quit on simple logic: Estimated expenses far outweighed projected income. That's no way to run a business. We were going down the tubes before we opened shop.

One month before we were to open our day care center we had in our hands only fourteen signed contracts generating a weekly income of $409. Since our weekly payroll would be $425 and our lunch and snack costs approximately $75, we were looking at a deficit of $91 per week. To make matters worse, two of those committed fourteen children moved from the district. The hard, cold reality of expenses outweighing the income became clearer to me with each passing Summer day.

A perfectionist by nature, I was finding possible defeat very tough to consider. There appeared to be no way out of the situation except to admit that a public district could not operate a day care program without Federal, State, or local taxpayer dollars.

No wonder no one else in our state was attempting such an idealistic project. It was a crazy idea.

It was a humbling experience—very painful.

I shared my unhappy data with the Superintendent. He very calmly suggested we scrap the idea. He expressed disappointment but not disappointment in me and I felt proud once again to be associated with him as a partner in public education. We truly did not want to begin an educational program that would fail financially and cause problems for the parents and children we intended to help. Our goal was not to be "first" in day care. Our goal was to be helpful to parents and children. If we couldn't be sure about reaching this goal, we'd have to abandon it.

Of course, Stubborn is my middle name. I began reassessing things and several options became viable.

(1) We could commit ourselves to offering day care for those 12 contracted Kindergarten children and simply hope to add a minimum of 6 more children by August 29. In other words, operate on faith and hope because "charity" was not one of our options.

(2) We could advertise before and after school care to first and second graders, thus enabling us to meet our weekly expenses.

(3) We could consider opening eight to ten slots to four-

year-olds but these would have to be full-time slots in order to generate maximum income. By moving to a mixed-age grouping, we would need staff members on duty to care for the four-year-olds while the five-year-olds were in Kindergarten.

I presented these three options to the Superintendent. He liked options 1 and 2 so we decided to wait another week before choosing a single plan of action.

Waiting another week did it!

The phone began ringing and never stopped. By August 22 we were putting Kindergarten parents on a waiting list. Option #1 took over without our having officially chosen it.

Twenty-three Kindergarteners enrolled in our day care program. Sixteen are "full-time" and seven are "part-time." We are licensed for 20 children which means we may care for no more than 20 children *at one time.* We were careful to assess the children's in and out time so that no more than 20 children would ever be in the room at the same time for child care.

Twenty-three parents would pay us a total of $570 per week. We would be able to meet our payroll, pay our cafeteria bills, and contribute toward the school's utility expenses. We would also be able to purchase supplies although we continued to depend heavily on donations from the community.

Weeding, worrying, and wondering disappeared into thin air, leaving behind the joy of nurturing.

Hindsight is a clarifying teacher. I now see where my thinking led me astray. In the future, my Monday morning quarterbacking will serve me well. If I can help other public or private educators avoid the agony I experienced during the Summer of '83, I'll feel good. Sharing successes is easy and helpful but sharing frustrations and near-failures may be more beneficial to others in the long run. Our district learned a great deal through my mistakes. Let's look at my major goofs.

Here's where I think I went astray. As a parent, I always planned and organized things for my kids long before implementation time. I never waited until the last minute in regard to any of my children's activities. Day Care was something foreign to me because I never needed it while my children were growing up. However, *had* I needed day care services, I would have arranged for them *months* before I needed them. As a result, I transferred *my* traits and priorities to all parents and came up with faulty assumptions. I should have known better than to assume anything. Murphy's Law is always at work!

A second area of enlightenment is that most parents in need of day care shop around for the least expensive program. Depending on a parent's income, marital status, and job location, child care is often selected on the basis of cost and convenience, not quality. I assumed parents would automatically choose *quality* over cost.

Another faulty assumption.

Parents with their financial and emotional backs against the wall *must* base decisions on dollars. I'd much prefer quality to be the deciding factor but I will never judge another person's decision-making unless I have walked at least twenty miles in her mocassins. Coping with everyday life is difficult for today's parents.

While I knew our day care costs were lower than most high quality day care services in our county, I was aware of a handful of centers offering care for $5 to $10 less per week. When a single mother (or father) inherits full responsibility for raising children and running a household, $5 or $10 a week is a significant amount. For a financially and emotionally overburdened parent, $5 or $10 extra a week can mean the difference between treading water or sinking.

And so, I had to learn the hard way that many veteran day care parents tend to procrastinate as well as shop around.

The telephone that continued to ring between August 15 and 29 was all the proof I needed.

Keep all of this in mind if you are as green and idealistic as I was during the various stages of our day care project. Today's "older" educator needs to sweep away personal values and priorities when exploring child care and today's parent and family.

On August 22 we held an inservice session for our day care staff. I arrived early in the morning with a jug of iced tea and a plate of shortbread. As I looked around the day care room, a feeling of peace flooded my innards. For the first time I recognized the reality of what we were accomplishing. We had indeed created a home-away-from-home. Our center would be unlike any other I had visited. It would be the best we could come up with for today's child. While the business end of day care was very difficult and challenging, the "educational" end of day care was cake!

The Department of Welfare requires a detailed description of program and staffing plans. Here is the way we met programming and staffing data requirements:

Plan of Daily Activities and Routines

Wilson's Day Care Center will be open Monday through Friday from 6:30 A.M. to 5:30 P.M. beginning August 29, 1983. Twenty children will be involved in this program.

Since *all* our day care children will be Kindergarteners, the most structured part of the day will be during the 2½ hour Kindergarten program.

Here is our projected daily plan:

6:30 A.M. to 8 A.M.—Children begin arriving. They play in the quiet area, rest if they are still sleepy, and/or have juice if they need it.

8 A.M. to 9 A.M.—Stories, coloring, talking time

9 A.M. to 10 A.M.—Large muscle activities, singing, and dancing

10 A.M. to 11 A.M.—Outdoors for an enjoyable, healthy walk. Play on playground after walk. If weather is bad, children will play in center.

11 A.M.–Lunch—A hot lunch will be served. Sometimes children will eat in the center and other times in the cafeteria.

11:30 A.M.—Rest time

11:50 A.M.—Clean-up time. Everyone helps to put everything in its place before going to Kindergarten.

12 NOON to 2:30 P.M.—Kindergarten

2:30 P.M. to 5:30 P.M.—Free choice will prevail. Some children will need to rest after Kindergarten. Others will choose to play with blocks, puzzles, and other manipulatives. Some will enjoy story time or arts and crafts projects.

Parents will begin picking up their children at intervals between 3:00 and 5:30 P.M.

The following room arrangement is being planned:

(1) A home-like concept will guide our room arrangement. It is our desire to de-institutionalize the center so it appears to be more like "home" than school. Unanimity reigns among Wilson District educators in this regard. Philosophically, we believe a Kindergarten day care center should not replicate a Kindergarten classroom.

(2) A "living room" will dominate one area of the center. A sofa or two, a comfortable chair, a rocker or two, an end table, a table lamp, and a bookcase, books, and magazines will be placed in this living room area.

(3) A gross motor area will be set up in a corner along the window and an inside wall.

(4) A "play" kitchen will be set up next to the gross motor area.

(5) A quiet play area will be created next to the living room. This area will house puzzles, art supplies, and other

manipulatives emphasizing fine motor exploration. A table and chairs will be available for children who choose to use them.

Staff Qualifications and Functions

One certified elementary teacher and three assistants will be hired by June 15, 1983. The certified teacher will be referred to as "Group Supervisor." One assistant will be "Assistant Group Supervisor" and two will be Aides.

The certified teacher will reveal a genuine love of young children and demonstrate an applicable understanding of the needs of five- and six-year-olds. The teacher will also be able to assume leadership, supervise aides, develop lesson plans, deal warmly and effectively with parents, maintain attendance records, and compile other pertinent data.

The Assistant Group Supervisor will assume a leadership role in the absence of the certified teacher. He/she will carry out the plans of the Supervisor.

Aides will be hired to maintain optimal adult–child ratios.

Aides and the assistant group supervisor will express a genuine love of children and demonstrate a warmth and acceptance of others. Aides will assist the group supervisor with children's activities as well as carry out the daily plans developed by the supervisor.

Aides and the assistant group supervisor might be certified teachers. They also might be adults who did not graduate from high school. Human quality is the most important qualification of day care employees.

High school students will be taking part in our day care activities during the morning hours. These students will receive training as volunteer aides and will be supervised by the home economics teacher and the high school principal.

A lab school concept will be attempted in our day care center. Our goal is to create an environment that is rich in positive learnings for both young children and high school students.

The Early Childhood Supervisor will be considered Director of Day Care and will oversee the planning and operation of the program.

Our "donations" appeal to the community did not fall on deaf ears. During the month of August we accepted donations of sofas, chairs, rockers, tables, lamps, toys, a refrigerator, rugs, bookcases, bulletin boards, and other assorted equipment and furniture. Our industrial arts supervisor built a neat sandbox for the children. Our center was truly a child's world.

We did not spend one penny of taxpayer money on our day care project. This was my most gratifying thought as I ran my hand over the back of the blue sofa. Establishing an educationally excellent day care center that would pay its own way was indeed possible within a public school district. In one more week, we'd be doing just that.

We were able to purchase art supplies with the $5 registration fee paid by each parent. This registration fee was also used for inservice coverage.

A few minutes later our four day care staff members began arriving. As I looked at each one, I knew we had chosen winners. Each was a warm and child-oriented adult. Each would bring special talent and love to our children.

How did we select four super staff members?

Read on.

Nurturing, Growing

Sometimes in public education we rush to hire teachers and other staff members before we develop a mental picture of the kind of people we want and need for our children.

Every new job opening in public education should be perceived as a golden opportunity to nurture in our continuing quest for excellence.

The moment the word was out about our district's *intention* to establish a day care program, the telephone rang off the desk. The calls were from people interested in day care *jobs*. We began receiving calls six months before we advertised for day care positions. By the time we *did* advertise, we had a telephone list of 60 candidates who wanted application forms.

It was becoming clear that we were unwittingly creating an unmanageable situation and that we would never have time to interview all interested applicants. Of course, it is not surprising we were flooded with inquiries. In this era of high unemployment coupled with mother's need for income, it is logical that women would gravitate toward children in seeking jobs. All inquiries for day care jobs came from women. Again, my candid assessment is that men did not apply because it is a known fact that day care salaries are relatively low.

It is unfair and it is wrong that early childhood employees persist and exist at the bottom of the pay scale. We made up our minds early in our explorations that we would pay our day care employees more than minimum wage. We knew we couldn't pay them as much as we'd like to but we were determined to go beyond minimum.

Of course, a district must examine many factors before setting day care salaries.

Because we were establishing a Kindergarten Day Care, these were our projected day care hours:

6:30 A.M. to 12 NOON	Day Care
12 NOON to 2:30 P.M.	Kindergarten Class
2:30 P.M. to 5:30 P.M.	Day Care

Theoretically, our day care center was open eleven hours a day. However, by scheduling all the day care children for afternoon Kindergarten, we were able to eliminate a need for day care staff during Kindergarten sessions. In practice, then, we needed to pay staff for 8½ hours a day. We could have our two morning staff members work until NOON and then have our afternoon staff begin at 2:30 P.M. when Kindergarten sessions were over.

Eventually, we decided it would be better to have our P.M. staff arrive at 2 P.M. in order to plan activities and be well-prepared to receive the children at 2:30.

We also decided our day care supervisor should begin at 6:30 A.M. and work until NOON. Our morning aide would begin at 7 A.M. and work until NOON, also.

Once we had our time frame formalized, we could begin *projecting* salaries.

This is how our staff looked, hours-wise:

Day Care Supervisor would work from 6:30 A.M. to 12 NOON five days a week. Supervisor would be paid for additional hours spent on staff development meetings twice-a-month.

The morning aide would work from 7 A.M. to 12 NOON five days a week for a total of 25 hours.

Two afternoon aides would work from 2 P.M. to 5:30 P.M. five days a week. Each would work 17½ hours for a total of 35 hours.

Total person hours per week equalled 89.

Next step was to estimate income (although we had fiddled with income ideas for months). We decided to consider 20 day care children at an average income of $30 each per week. If our projected income was $600 per week, we decided we could come up with the following hourly rates for staff:

Supervisor would receive $6 per hour.
Each aide would receive $4 per hour.

Remember, we were establishing a non-profit day care center so we wanted to break even, monetarily. However, we had expenses other than payroll so we had to make sure we had enough income for children's lunches and snacks as well as supplies, equipment, and utility and rental contributions.

We decided to commit ourselves to the hourly rates of $6 and $4. The letters (which can be seen in the Appendix) were then mailed to day care *supervisor* applicants and day care *aide* applicants.

These letters proved to be mighty helpful in "weeding out" candidates *before* interviews were set up. Applicants who needed more working hours or a higher hourly rate simply chose not to schedule an interview.

As it was, 8 supervisor candidates and 12 aide candidates were "screened" for interviews.

Interview dates and times were scheduled with our four elementary Principals. After all candidates were interviewed initially, the Principals narrowed the supervisor field to 3 and the aide candidates to 7.

The Superintendent and I were to interview these ten candidates and make decisions by June 1.

A great deal of nurturing and growing was taking place long before we selected our Supervisor and her three aides. As a public school district, we were concerned about fully informing the entire Wilson community—residents and school employees as well. *Sunshine*, our monthly early childhood parent newsletter and *Wilson's Pride*, the District's monthly newsletter became our major form of written communication.

Faculty meetings and, of course, telephone inquiries became ways to get our verbal messages across.

Whenever planning for innovative educational trail blazing, it's wise to prepare district residents *and* district employees. Each group deserves equal respect and attention.

We communicated well and often because we believe:

An informed community is a prepared community.

An informed faculty is an accepting faculty.

An inform*ing* district is a wise district.

Selecting a day care Supervisor and three aides was both difficult and easy. The Principals selected excellent candidates. The Superintendent and I interviewed these final candidates and made our recommendations to the Board of Education.

We were now less than three months away from opening day.

Not Ready, Not Set, But Go

Sometimes I silently wondered how a labor of love could produce so much anxiety. The closer we inched toward day care reality, the more complicated everything became.

I had figured the toughest part was behind us as we approached the middle of August. It had been a kind of euphoric day on August 9 when the representative from the Department of Welfare assured us we'd be granted a provisional certificate. As mentioned earlier, we met immediately all but two regulations. I had to write justifications for noncompliance in these two cases.

Regarding no screens at the windows, I wrote that:

(1) Safety was not a factor since our center is located on the first floor.
(2) The windows are casement-type windows and special box screens would have to be made—a costly item.
(3) The window opening does not exceed six inches.
(4) Lunch would not be eaten in the day care room so insects would not be attracted by food.
(5) Windows would be opened for ventilation only.

In regard to having no telephone in the day care room, I originally thought the intercom system would be an acceptable substitute. The day care parents would have to call the

67

Whitfield office, the secretary would buzz day care on the intercom and the day care staff could get the parent's message via intercom. No problem.

However, I neglected to consider what would happen in case a parent needed to contact day care *after* the school secretary left for the day. The hours between 4 and 5:30 P.M. became the issue. Obviously, the Department of Welfare had a valid reason for asking us to comply with the telephone regulations or come up with an acceptable compromise. The Department of Welfare would allow us four weeks to solve this problem.

The Superintendent first conferred with our Business Manager who immediately checked out the possibility of installing a phone in the day care room. Cost became a prohibitive feature. The Business Manager discovered that installation at the day care end of the building would be a major job, costing in the neighborhood of $500.

Undaunted, the Superintendent moved on to Plan B. (Sometimes he drives people crazy with his endless supply of alternative plans.) He telephoned the Whitfield secretary and asked her if she would like to begin her working day a half hour later and end it a half hour later. She said that would suit her just fine as long as her morning clerical aide could cover things in the office between 7:30 and 8 A.M. The secretary called the aide and then she called the Superintendent informing him that the aide agreed to begin her day a half-hour earlier.

We were very grateful to the secretaries. Now we still had to solve the problem of telephone coverage between 4:30 and 5:30 P.M.

The Superintendent considered having a bell installed in the day care center that could be activated for that hour each afternoon. We could advise parents to let the phone ring and ring until a day care aide could reach the school office and answer the phone.

I made a list of the children who were still in day care between 4:30 and 5:30 P.M. Six children fell into this category. We were ready to go with the bell idea and inform those six parents and then the Superintendent came up with Plan C.

Plan C called for assigning the Whitfield custodian to the office area at 4:30 each day. As the custodian cleaned the offices, she would answer any incoming telephone calls. We wrote a waiver, explaining our intended solution.

The problem was solved.

The Department of Welfare approved the Superintendent's Plan C.

We now complied with all but one regulation. The Department of Welfare would review our waiver request regarding screens at the windows. In the meantime, we were given the go-ahead to open our center, as planned, on August 29.

But August 29 was still two weeks away. Just when some of the anxieties were diffusing, my office telephone began ringing more than usual. Some of our day care parents had job changes or shift changes and needed to rearrange day care service. A few parents were laid off and weren't sure whether or not they'd be able to commit themselves to day care monetarily until they were sure of employment.

The confusion grew and grew until I was absolutely certain I had made a terrible mistake. Here I was, a non-business person, running a business with no operating capital, no "seed" money, and not enough projected income to pay projected expenses.

The moment of truth was upon me. I felt defeated and was ready to throw in our towel until I realized that when you attempt to run a business without any "seed" money, you can't even buy a towel.

I headed for the Assistant Superintendent's office. The Assistant Superintendent is a calm, quiet listener. A year before he patiently convinced me our district could run its own day care center without help from anyone else. I needed to hear him say those words again.

He did. I believed him again. He was right.

Over the next few days, we received new enrollees for day care and rearranged payment plans for parents whose day care needs changed. During those two weeks before we opened our day care doors, our projected income figure changed dozens and dozens of times. Green as grass, business-wise, I found this phenomenon petrifying. In retrospect, I see it as just a day care fact of life. I had simply overreacted. After four months of operation, little fazes me in regard to the ever-changing world of day care.

As I say several times a month, "In day care, the only constant is change."

We orderly traditionalists are working overtime as we learn to look at the educational world through different eyes. The next decade will exist only for those public educators who are willing to trade in myopia for farsightedness.

Ah, but it's tough.

Then again, nobody is saying it's going to be easy. Establishing a high quality, low cost, educationally sound day care center in the public schools is quite a challenge. One person alone cannot do it. The whole district has to work as a team. With teamwork, *any* public district can operate its own day care program without Federal, State, or local funds.

Day Care payments started rolling in a week before our center opened. We asked parents to pay one week in advance. We considered that one week advance their security deposit. In case a parent fell behind in payments or abruptly withdrew a child from day care without notice, the security deposit would cover our expenses. A day care center must plan for the possible or the unforeseeable in order to survive. In line with this thinking, we asked parents to sign a contract with us, agreeing that if they fell one week behind in payments, day care services could be terminated. We weren't being mean. We were encouraging parents to be responsible as parents.

Happily, after four months of operation, all parents have been paying on time. That's the way it ought to be. But just in case, that security deposit will be our insurance policy. And our gentle "Oops" reminder is waiting patiently in a desk drawer . . . just in case we need it.

The business end of our day care venture was finally beginning to make sense. And not a minute too soon.

August 29 arrived. To our terrific day care Supervisor and our terrific aides all we could say was:

Get Ready, Get Set, Go.

Smoother Sailing

Hire a superior day care staff. Coordinate children's day care schedules with the Kindergarten teachers. Appreciate everything the Whitfield Principal does for you. Appreciate everybody's help. Smile when people ask if you're ready for day care. Order sand for the sandbox. Attempt to buy a fan to fight the heat wave. Discover every fan in the county has been sold. Borrow a fan from the school nurse. Borrow two aspirins as well. Get a receipt book for the Whitfield secretary. Appreciate her willingness to handle all day care payments. Buy polaroid film. Forget flashbulbs. Go back and buy flashbulbs. Scrounge for art supplies. Order juice, raisins, and crackers for snacks. Thank the Assistant Superintendent for arranging the loan of a refrigerator for one year. Thank the Business Manager and his assistant for setting up a day care account with the promise of instant feedback whenever income or expense data are needed. Thank the Superintendent and his wife for donating a sofa and chair. Thank the Superintendent's daughter for donating a bulletin board. Feel grateful our day care supervisor is recuperated from her recent tonsilectomy. Gather health records of all the children. Buy geraniums for the windowsills. Decide on a day care logo.

Remember to forget to worry.

Day Care is in good and caring hands.

Remember once again how good it is to work for and with public educators who *listen.* Recall earlier conversations with the Superintendent and Assistant Superintendent when day care was less than the seed of an idea.

We would go round and round, questioning, arguing, compromising, agreeing, and weighing our own personal philosophies against the needs of today's child and parent. There were some mighty tough issues to come to grips with before we could even address the Board on day care. One such issue was the question of all-day Kindergarten.

Should we offer full-day Kindergarten programs for children whose parents work at jobs outside the home? The only way we could answer the question was to gather a variety of data. We met with Department of Education leaders to discuss the merits of full-day Kindergarten. At that time, districts were being encouraged to *consider* full-day programs for Kindergartens. In addition to meeting with our state's educational leaders, we gathered research done in this area. We also attended workshops and presentations that explored the full-day Kindergarten program.

Pooling our data and examining our feelings did not convince us that *most* five-year-olds are developmentally ready to *sustain or cope* with six hours of "instruction" in an educational setting.

Call us old-fashioned—that's O.K. with us—but our personal beliefs and our educational knowledge and experience would not allow us to choose full-day Kindergarten for our district's children. We felt a well-designed 2½ hour a day Kindergarten program guided by loving, well-qualified teachers was the best educational offering for our little ones. The only way I could personally accept our creation of a full-day Kindergarten program was if:

> The Department of Education would allow us to call such a program half-day Kindergarten and half-day day care.
>
> OR
>
> District-provided transportation for half-day Kindergarten classes becomes too costly.

We debated the full-day vs half-day issue for several weeks. Since our day care idea was educational virginity, our state Department of Education preferred a full-day Kindergarten program and was not quite ready for our combination Kindergarten-day care concept. We understood. There were no hard feelings. We just decided to hold fast to our beliefs and not yield to the contemporary premise that early formal education benefits children holistically. We believed in a half-day school curriculum and a half-day of "homeyness."

Sometimes you just have to stand up and be counted—even when your position is unpopular in some areas. When the all-around welfare of children is concerned, we need to resist the power of present trends—unless, of course, we happen to believe in them.

In this case, we did not believe in the educational soundness of a full day of Kindergarten "instruction."

We still don't. And until we can be convinced otherwise, we will not operate full-day Kindergartens.

Of course, the complexity and cost of offering bus transportation for half-day Kindergarten students can become prohibitive. If this burdens our district as it has burdened others, we may have to offer full-day Kindergarten sessions.

However, we will be truthful with the community if and when this situation arises. We will *not* suggest a full-day program is being created because it is educationally "right" for all our Kindergarteners. We will tell the community we believe in a half-day program but cannot afford the transportation costs such a program creates.

Our Assistant Superintendent studied transportation costs during those see-saw weeks and was able to convince us our district's transportation costs were not excessive and that operating half-day Kindergarten classes was not burdensome.

This became another key moment of truth. We believed in half-day Kindergarten instruction and we were convinced that bus transportation costs were absolutely affordable to our district.

A half-day Kindergarten and half-day Day Care Program, therefore, became our only acceptable, viable, educational plan.

Remember how this decision freed us to move forward with thoughtful swiftness. Remember for the hundredth time how good it is, indeed, to work for and with administrators, Board members, teachers, and parents who *listen* . . . and who support sound programs for the good of kids!

This whole day care preamble has been more bumpy than smooth. Believe once again that anything worth anything is usually founded on a challenging "preamble."

The first two days of day care enjoy rather smooth sailing (except for one lost child). Feel grateful you had the green luck to think to open day care two days before the new school year begins. Only eight children need our services those first two days. It helps us to "break in" without a full house.

On the first day of school—August 31—you forget to remember to forget to worry. Deciding to stay away from the Whitfield building on August 31 is a good idea. But watch the clock every seven minutes. Expect the phone to ring with emergency type news. Force yourself to meet the responsibilities of your life-work other than the day care program. Semi-succeed.

Look at the clock. Sigh with relief. Tell your aide and friend, Mary Long, that everything must have gone smoothly between day care and Kindergarten. It's 2:30 P.M. School's over. Some day care children are boarding a school bus for home. A few day care children are walking home. Most are returning to the day care room across the hall until their parents come to pick them up after work. The clock tells you your worries were unnecessary, as usual. Feel mad at yourself.

Answer the phone at 2:45. Hear the frantic voice of a day care mother asking why her son didn't get off the school bus. Speak to the mother in a calm, confident voice. Ask for her phone number. Promise to call her back in a few minutes. Assure her Billy is safe—somewhere.

Hang up the phone. Sweat. Imagine Billy anywhere but safe. Pick up the telephone. Call the Whitfield School. Ask for the Kindergarten teacher. Hear the Kindergarten teacher say Billy went home on the bus. Hang up. Sweat again. Call the transportation supervisor. Ask him to check with the driver of bus #5. Wait. Hear the transportation supervisor say Billy never got on Bus #5.

Hang up. Feel kind of sick. Pick up the phone again. Call the Whitfield building. Ask the secretary to check if Billy is in the day care center. Wait. Discover Billy is there! Find out Billy began heading for the bus and then decided this might be his after school day care day. Whisper thanks to the secretary. Tell her to keep Billy in the center. Hang up.

Call Billy's mother. Smile to her over the phone. Tell her Billy is safe and she can pick him up now. Chat happily for two more minutes.

Hang up.

Cry.

Feel good now.

Through The Eyes of The Superintendent

The authors of "A Nation at Risk" ought to visit our school district and meet our Superintendent. They would discover in us and in him the absence of a rising tide of mediocrity. Instead, the authors of "A Nation at Risk" would witness an orchestration of a rising crescendo of *excellence.*

The guy with the baton in his hand, leading our educational orchestra, is our Superintendent.

He can drive us crazy with Plans A, B, C, D, E and he can send us up the wall with his relentless pursuit of superior ways to solve problems. His missionary zeal for educational excellence will continue to gain him as many critics as supporters and both critic and supporter will continue to benefit from his visions.

Never at a loss for words, our Superintendent on many occasions expressed his opposition to the concept of day care. To this day, he is not an advocate of the day care movement in the United States. How, then, did his district become the first in Pennsylvania to establish and operate its own day care center?

Dr. Dubelle can tell you in his own words.

Here's what he has to say:

"Day Care! Who needs it! I believe at least three groups do, the most important of whom is the group of children whose parents *need* to work and cannot care for their children during daytime hours. The other two groups are the parents who cannot care for their children because they choose to be engaged elsewhere during the day; the final group is the professional educators, the ones who must educate the children of day care.

"Before explaining my position on the above three groups, let me say that I do not think day care is an idea whose time should have come, but it did. It's undeniably with us. Ignoring it won't make it go away; cussing and discussing it won't make it go away. Saying it's someone else's headache won't make it any better. Raising one's eyes toward the heavens and outstretching one's arms while saying, 'Not another one! We can't take on one more of society's problems!' won't make things better. It is an undeniable movement.

"Since day care is with us and we know we can't make it go away, why doesn't public education join the movement? Joining does not mean we have to embrace whatever virtues the advocates claim for day care. Contrariwise, joining the movement does not mean we must construct a Trojan Horse from which we launch attacks against the movement. To us, joining meant getting involved to the extent that *if* children were going to be put in day care "places," then we would like to make the places as wholesome and home-like as possible. We would be doing this for the future students of our school district.

"We would also like to do our part in showing others how the care of children can be done in a non-institutionalizing way and how children can have their earlier lives enriched rather than impoverished. In this way, we are joining the movement, even if we don't believe in it in the first place. We are making it better for children, as well as those parents

77

who genuinely have no other alternatives for the care of their children. That group of parents are the ones who truly must be away from the home during the day so that they can provide the basic essentials for living.

"In the relatively brief time day care has been in existence, we have seen enough to know that in all the places where day care exists, there is not always quality care. In our school district, we have been seeing more and more children being enrolled in our kindergarten and first grades coming out of a mold that has cast them into a confused, bewildered state. In four words, there is "a lack of readiness." The readiness for school that was once developed by parents in the settings of the living room, the kitchen, the garage, the cellar or attic, and the backyard of the home was becoming more and more infrequent. Proper development of children was lacking. In its place we saw vapid stares. Some children looked as though they hadn't blinked their eyes for three years. Others displayed the opposite behavior. They were aggressive, angry, and often volatile. Institutionalization and the shuttling of these children among four or five different "sitters" a week had been taking their toll.

"As for the parents, we saw an entrapment. Those who genuinely needed care for their children were experiencing a debilitating guilt that was eating at their relationship with their children. Parents were tense from their guilt and they were transferring the tenseness to their children in the form of shortness, uneasiness, impatience, and the like. Parents needed the reassurance and the tangible evidence that their children were indeed in good places.

"How can it be that educators need day care? We all know that preventative actions are far better than remedial ones. As public educators, we found ourselves, more and more, in the remediation business. We knew that if we didn't do something, and do it right, we were deciding to doom ourselves to a Sisyphus role of repeating, interminably and unsuccessfully, the remediation of what could never be remediated, readiness to learn. We decided not to play Sisyphus."

So there you have it—through the eyes of a Superintendent. Our Superintendent.

A listener, for sure!

Of course, his ending is a little Greek to me.

Where Do We Go From Here?

The Wilson District has a student population of 3,800. Approximately 10,000 people live within the district's geographical parameters. It may be difficult to believe, but no one publicly opposed our day care project. As far as I know, the district received no telephone calls or letters criticizing our new venture.

We can probably attribute this lack of opposition to several things:

(1) The need for day care services spans all walks of life. Day care need is no longer "owned" by the poor, single parent. Day care now belongs to every social class and every family structure. Many Wilson parents need day care. The Wilson District needs students to educate. A marriage of Kindergarten and Day Care makes sense to a lot of people, especially when taxpayer money is *not* being used.

(2) The Superintendent, Assistant Superintendent, and Board of Education members decided unanimously to pursue the project. The importance of unanimity among Board members and administrators is vital when inviting a socially sensitive issue under the umbrella of public education. Quite simply, we spoke in one voice. I like the sound we make when we speak for children in one voice.

(3) The district openly communicated the day care idea with teachers, parents, and the community-at-large. We prepared everyone as fully as possible through newsletters, meetings, and cable television.

And so, after planting seeds, hoeing, weeding, worrying, nurturing, and experiencing many mood swings, we're feeling pretty good about where we are today. Where do we go from here? Well, in all honesty, we don't have to go anywhere from here. Things are evolving nicely and our new status quo is enticing to pursue. We could enjoy another year with one day care center in operation.

Status quo, however, will not help the quality of day care or public education. Besides, our beautiful day care staff is providing such excellent care for 23 of our children, we are being asked by the community to expand.

At the moment we are exploring a number of expansion possibilities. Here are our expansion ideas. Remember, they are ideas, not promises. We can't possibly take on all the child care needs of the community but we can do more than we are doing presently.

We are looking into:

(1) A Summertime day care program for primary grade children—K–3

(2) An additional Kindergarten day care center for the next school year

(3) Before and after school day care for young elementary students.

Parents are in the process of returning to us a new questionnaire regarding the above three expansion ideas. A sample of the questionnaire is in the Appendix section.

Only time and reevaluation will tell which way we'll go. There is no pressure from Board or Administration to expand unless we feel we can create outstanding programs for children and their parents.

Here's an expansion idea for other districts. Why not consider turning one of your white elephant type school buildings into an early childhood center? Several day care centers could be created with mixed-age groupings. You could open day care services to three- or four-year-olds as well as Kindergarten age children. In order to eliminate excessive need for busing little ones, establish a Kindergarten or two in this early childhood building. Day Care Kindergarteners could walk down the hall to Kindergarten class and then return to day care afterward—on foot and under one roof.

Our district philosophy includes a belief in half-day Kindergarten and half-day Day Care. A full-day Kindergarten program was studied but not pursued. As a former Kindergarten teacher, I have a personal bias about Kindergarten rooms and day care rooms being different. I suppose I could live with the idea of Kindergarten and day care being experienced in the same room but I'd have trouble believing it is best for the children. I see Kindergarten as school and day care as home-away-from-home. Separation of the two works very, very well for us at Wilson. Besides, how many adults enjoy spending up to eleven hours a day in one room, five days a week?

Another idea for your white elephant type school is before and after school day care for elementary students, K–6. This kind of program could open up jobs for residents of the district. I like the idea of creating employment for residents of the district. It's kind of like looking out for your neighbor. Day Care staff could be hired from within the community. The more community involvement in day care, the more successful the program will be. There is pride in ownership, and the community, through the school, "owns" day care.

Volunteers from the community can help keep the adult–child ratio ideal. Coordination of a volunteer system takes time and lots of organizational skills. Day care volunteerism can work only if it is well-coordinated.

In October, we began a student volunteer program for our Kindergarten Day Care center. Student volunteers must be at least fifteen-years-old. Three of us coordinated things—the day care supervisor, a senior high home economics teacher, and I. Each morning, four high school seniors come to day care for 1½ hours. The students have specific things to do with and for the children and they are in love with the program. Each day four different high school students participate. In that way, we are able to involve 20 Wilson seniors. The potential benefits to both Kindergartener and teen-ager are obvious. So far this program is working well.

On Friday afternoons, one of Wilson's learning disabled teen-agers assists the aides with activities for the children. This cooperative effort is rewarding at both ends. We reach out to include all child-oriented partners in our day care family.

Another idea for public districts is to consider renting empty classrooms to private day care centers. This might be a good way to ease into the world of day care before tackling the project yourself. Our district is presently renting a large room to a woman who operates a day care center for children between the ages of 3 and 5. We charge a monthly rental fee of $350. This center is not located in the elementary school where our district-operated center is housed. One major advantage to our district is the fact that five of our Kindergarteners are cared for in this private day care center before and after Kindergarten. No busing is necessary and we like this arrangement for the children and for us. Our enrollment increased as a result of this rental of space.

We rent another room to our county's Intermediate Unit for a Title XX day care program. This Title XX day care center is located in an elementary building that does not have Kindergarten classes. In this case, a van transports the Title XX Kindergarteners to and from Kindergarten classes in another building.

By operating our own day care program, we are providing services for 23 Kindergarten children, all Wilson residents.

By renting a classroom to a private day care center, we are adding five more Kindergarteners to our Kindergarten program.

By renting a classroom to a government sponsored Title XX program, we are including 7 additional Kindergarteners to our Kindergarten program.

If we were not providing services and "space" to Kindergarteners in day care, we estimate we would lose the majority of these 35 children to out-of-the-district private all-day Kindergartens.

Parents who work outside the home *and* outside the district usually find day care services near their place of employment.

This is one reason so many public districts are experiencing a decline in Kindergarten enrollment. If child care for Kindergarteners is not available in the district in which they live, parents will seek child care and school *outside* the district.

Some of the children a district loses as Kindergarteners will return the next year for first grade. However, many do not return. They continue their education elsewhere. And, as mentioned earlier, children who do not receive a district's Kindergarten program often experience adjustment difficulties as district first graders.

Establishing day care in public school gives parents the

opportunity to choose their district's public Kindergarten for their children.

Parents have been telling us for years they wanted to send their children to public Kindergarten but had no choice except to seek private day care or all-day Kindergarten outside the district.

Our goal is not to compete with private day care. Our goal is to offer a high quality, low cost program as a *choice*. Our district's parents will make the decision for their children. Free choice prevails.

Where do we go from here is an organic, creative question. We can go as far as we want to go in public education.

The sky's the limit as long as the stars we reach for are children.

The sky's the limit as long as our thinking precedes our action. Our developmental creations for young children need to be "right" and good and appropriate and lasting.

The sky's the limit for public education as we explore this decade.

It's now or never.

The End, A New Beginning

This is the end of our "How to . . . " handbook, which is to say, the beginning for other public educators.

However, in education there is never an ending—only new beginnings. Even for us at Wilson, day care will be "new" next year. Our latest parent questionnaire (the one that appears in the Appendix section) continues to arrive from anxious, hopeful parents who see our day care program as the solution to their family's #1 problem.

It may be difficult for most Americans to comprehend the magnitude of child care problems—especially people who grew up in the 1940's and '50's. It is a world unlike any "social" world this country has ever seen.

While we at Wilson certainly understand it better, we may never understand it fully. It is likely we will never achieve total understanding. Our district, however, has a clearly defined philosophy regarding early childhood education and parenting.

I believe we understand the all-around needs of little people and big people. These all-around needs are compounded by the phenomenon of day care. Parents of children under six years of age need all-day child care. Parents of school age children need before and after school care. The demand for child care is far greater than existing day care centers, neighbors, relatives, and sitters can handle.

Why not establish day care centers in our public schools?

Pie in the sky?

Worming our way in where we don't belong?

Taking over the responsibility of parents and families?

Taking over the role of the church?

Biting off more than we can chew?

Obviously, you heard these persuasive arguments before. In fact, you read them in the foreword to this handbook.

If, upon reading them the second time, you feel dead set against exploring day care in public schools, forget the idea . . . at least for awhile. It's no crime to feel uncomfortable with a new idea.

The funny thing is, I still have a wrestler's hold on past values and a nostalgic yearning to inject today's family with the "old way" of having one loving parent at home during a preschooler's waking hours.

I still do not believe in the *concept* of day care. I still do not believe an institutional social environment is as wholesome for the young child as a warm family setting. A child's first social group has historically been family. I'm not sure we'll like some of the consequences of day care centers being the first social group for many children.

I still believe early separation from parents—especially Mother—can have long-term repercussions as the child matures.

Of course, only time will tell whether or not my concerns are valid. In the meantime, however, our district will work to continue creating a home-like environment for our day care children. We will continue to employ adults who genuinely love children. Our day care staff can never replace parents in the lives of children but our staff will provide ideal adult models for children to emulate.

Today's young child often spends more waking hours with child care adults than he does with parents in a family setting. Because of this common occurrence of the 1980's, today's young child needs to be with gentle, caring, mentally healthy adults during his waking hours.

Public education just might be able to open those caring arms in ways that will benefit everyone—children, parents, teachers, administrators, and the community-at-large.

The Day Care question is for everybody. Former President Gerald Ford said those words in a recent article in *Parade.* Important, internationally influential males don't often address the day care issue. The fact that a former President did so is attention-getting.

Public educators can be those who follow suit. We may not be internationally influential but we certainly enjoy some local influence. Many communities are ready to explore day care in public school. If *you* are ready to explore this possibility, let's review the steps that helped us reach our goal. Consider this review a checklist.

STEP 1 ☐ Do your homework

STEP 2 ☐ Address the Board of Education

STEP 3 ☐ Survey the community

STEP 4 ☐ Assess community needs

Stop here if needs assessment indicates your community does not have day care needs

STEP 5 ☐ Get Board approval for one-year pilot program

STEP 6 ☐ Develop more specific parent questionnaire for parents who responded to community questionnaire

STEP 7 ☐ Study parent response and analyze needs, expenses, and projected income

STEP 8 ☐ Contact Department of Welfare and Department of Labor and Industry

STEP 9 ☐ Write two or three proposals. Consider Kindergarten day care, mixed-age groupings, and before and after school day care programs

STEP 10 ☐ Study buildings, rooms, and other physical aspects of establishing a day care center

STEP 11 ☐ Decide which Day Care Proposal to activate and decide on Day Care location

STEP 12 ☐ Explore staffing needs and salaries

STEP 13 ☐ Ask community for furniture

STEP 14 ☐ Advertise for Day Care Supervisor and Aides

STEP 15 ☐ Interview and select Day Care staff

STEP 16 ☐ Send contracts to parents who pre-registered for day care

STEP 17 ☐ Use registration fees for Day Care Staff Inservice

STEP 18 ☐ Meet all requirements of Department of Welfare and Department of Labor and Industry and receive provisional license

STEP 19 ☐ Open Day Care Center

STEP 20 ☐ Evaluate continuously

And so public education just may be within reach of something special—something community-spirited— something educationally exciting. Day Care in the public schools just might give public education the morale boost it so badly needs. Enrollment is bound to increase, as well.

Who is raising America's children is a question of interest to all of us. But there is a more important question we need to be asking. *How* are we raising America's children?

It does little good to lament the fact that things are very different for today's family. Lamenting is never forward-moving or problem-solving. Instead it saps our energy and prevents us from rolling up our sleeves and getting to work—for the good of children, parents, public education, and communities.

When 3 million married women joined the "working" world during World War II, the day care concept was born. Thousands of children needed care outside the home. By 1990, it is projected that more than 10½ million children under age six will need to be cared for outside the home. The day care snowball will have been rolling for fifty years by 1990.

Will public education continue to roll away from the day care issue?

Public education is in serious trouble if it continues to withdraw from the day care snowball in fear, anger, ignorance, or disgust.

Child care in the United States is everybody's concern.

The consequences of doing nothing are scarier than the consequences of doing something that appears a little risky.

This is public education's decade for coming out of the closet and revealing its true identity as a caring profession in continuous pursuit of excellence. Public education is in the process of renewing itself in many ways.

Establishing day care centers is just one form of renewal. It's working for us.

It can work for others.

And now we've got to end our printed exploration of day care. You see, in three weeks we're going to open our second day care center. From the looks of things, we'll probably have another story to tell.

APPENDICES

A completion of sample forms, letters, and information
sheets for the use of School Districts planning their own Day
Care Program are shown on the following pages.

_____ SCHOOL DISTRICT

November, 19___

DAY CARE NEEDS FOR PARENTS OF KINDERGARTENERS AND 4-YEAR-OLDS

If your child will be registering for our district's Kindergarten program and if you will be in need of child care, we want you to know we are LOOKING INTO starting a Day Care Program for Kindergarten children beginning September 19___ .

We are also LOOKING INTO starting a Day Care Program for 4-year-olds. (Children *must* be 4 by September 30, 19___ .)

Before we can make any definite plans, we need to hear from you. After you read the following information, please fill out the QUESTIONNAIRE and return it to us by December 15.

If we offer a program, it will include a half-day Kindergarten class and half-day Day Care for 5-year-olds and full-day Day Care for 4-year-olds. Planned activities, hot lunch, and rest time would be part of this program. The question of transportation would have to be explored with you on an individual basis.

Cost for this Day Care Program (Kindergarten is free) would be comparable to other Day Care costs in Berks County. If we begin a Program, we assure you it will be excellent.

We personally believe parents, family, and home are more important than anything else during a child's early years. We are also aware that the 1980s are creating many changes in the lives of mothers and fathers and children. More than half of our mothers are now working at jobs outside the home. Also, one-parent families are increasing at a faster rate than most of us realize.

Times are changing. Even though we believe a young child grows best when he or she spends the preschool years in the care of loving family members, school districts need to begin accepting a share in the responsibility of caring for — and about — the young child in today's changing world. A district that opens caring arms *before* children begin formal schooling is a district that cares about the total well-being of all of its children.

By offering a Day Care Program for 4-year-olds and Kindergarteners, the District is, in effect, encouraging parents to *try* to give their preschoolers 3 to 4 years *at home* before seeking child care. Then if parents need to work outside the home, let us help families with their 4- and 5-year-olds. Make sense? We hope so!

We care. We really do.

Before we can make any definite decisions about beginning a Day Care Program, we need to hear from you. Please answer the questions on the back.

FRONT

92

QUESTIONNAIRE

Kindergarten Plus Day Care

I would be interested in our district's half-day Kindergarten and half-day Day Care Program beginning in September, 19___ . (Remember—children must be 5 by September 30, 19___ in order to be eligible for Kindergarten.)

Yes _____   No _____

My child would need to be cared for from _____ A.M. to _____ P.M.
(Please write in the total time child would be away from home.)

In which area of the District do you live? _____

DAY CARE FOR 4-YEAR-OLDS

I would be interested in Day Care for my 4-year-old.
(Children must be 4 by September 30, 19___ .)

5 days a week _____   On a part-time basis _____

My child would need to be cared for from _____ A.M. to _____ P.M.
(Please write in the total time child would be away from home.)

Please provide the following information:

Child's Name _____

Child's Birthdate _____

Parent's Name _____

Address _____   Phone No. (Home) _____

_____   (Work) _____

Please add any information which would be helpful to us.

Send QUESTIONNAIRE with a school-age child and save postage or mail on or before DECEMBER 15 to:

Early Childhood Supervisor
_____ School District
(Address)

BACK

93

PARENT QUESTIONNAIRE

Kindergarten-Day Care Program for the _____ **District**

1. I am still interested in a combination of Kindergarten and Day Care.

   _____ Yes   _____ No

2. I need Day Care five days a week.

   _____ Yes   _____ No

3. Day Care hours would probably operate from 6:30 A.M. to 5:30 P.M.

   My child would need to be cared for from _____ A.M. to _____ P.M.
   (Please write in the total time child would be away from home.)

4. Our Kindergarten program is 2½ hours. *(Kindergarten is free.)* Day Care costs would vary according to the needs of parents. There will be several cost-plans. These plans will probably range from $30–$45 a week. (This cost includes lunch.) This cost range is within my budget, and I will be able to pay this amount. (Our program will receive no funds from Federal, State, or local sources. Total cost of Day Care must be paid by the parents.)

   _____ Yes   _____ No

5. This program will operate from August 22 to June 30. This is acceptable to me.

   _____ Yes   _____ No

6. I wish to pre-register my child for our district's Kindergarten-Day Care Program.

   _____ Yes   _____ No

Child's Name _____ Child's Birthdate _____

Parent's Name _____

Address _____

Phone Number _____

Comments:

Please return as soon as possible to: Early Childhood Supervisor
                                        _____ School District
                                        (Address)

_____ SCHOOL DISTRICT

(address)

April 11, 19___

Dear Applicant:

We promised to communicate with you in April regarding your interest in day care employment. You expressed an interest in the position of Day Care Supervisor and completed an application form which we have on file. The following is for your information:

> Our Kindergarten-Day Care Program will begin August 22, 19___. One supervisor (a certified elementary teacher) and three aides will be hired.

> The supervisor will receive $6.00 per hour and will work from 6:30 A.M. to 12:15 P.M. for a total of 28¾ hours each week. One aide will work from 7:00 A.M. to 12 noon for a total of 25 hours each week. Two aides will work from 2:00 P.M. to 5:30 P.M. for a total of 17½ hours each week. Aides will receive $4.00 per hour. There will be no fringe benefits for either the supervisor or the aide positions.

> Our day care room will be in the _____ Elementary School. Children in day care will attend afternoon kindergarten at the _____ School (12 noon to 2:30 P.M.).

> Day care hours will be from 6:30 A.M. to 5:30 P.M., five days a week.

> It is probable that our Day Care Center will be open on bad weather days, even if the _____ School District cancels regular classes. Our day care policy is, "We never close." (Well, almost never!)

As you can imagine, the response to our day care concept has been tremendous. Since we have received more than 80 requests for day care employment, we will not be able to offer interviews to everyone. As a result of our being overwhelmed with applicants, a committee will screen applicants and decide to call twenty for interviews. All interviews will take place during the months of May and June. If you are one of the twenty chosen for an interview, you will hear from us by phone or by mail before May 13.

We certainly appreciate your enthusiastic interest in our new educational endeavor.

Sincerely,

Early Childhood Supervisor

QUESTIONS FOR DAY CARE APPLICANTS

Position of Day Care Supervisor

Applicant's Name _____ Date _____

(1) What does the term "Day Care" mean to you?

(2) Our Day Care children will be between 5 and 6 years of age. They will probably attend afternoon Kindergarten. What types of activities would you plan for them during the morning hours?

(3) How do you feel about overseeing and coordinating the work of 3 day care aides?

(4) The Supervisor will begin his or her day at 6:30 A.M. How do you feel about that? Would this present a problem? (Watch for nonverbals and make notes!!)

(5) The Supervisor would be responsible for *some* record keeping, such as children's attendance, aides' schedules, special needs, etc. Organizational skills and accuracy are very important. Would this be a problem to you?

(6) What kinds of experiences have you had with young children?

(7) Our Day Care program is guaranteed to operate until June 30. If the program is successful, we will operate it on a year-round basis. Are you interested in 12 month employment or do you prefer 9½ month employment?

(8) After reading the informational letter about our day care program, do you have any questions or concerns?

DAY CARE STAFF MEETING

September 9, 19____ at 1 P.M.

AGENDA

A. Personal Observations, Plus and Minus—Staffing
   (1) Day Care Supervisor
   (2) Aide #1
   (3) Aide #2
   (4) Aide #3
   (5) Day Care Administrator

B. The Children
   (1) Who has greatest needs?
   (2) How do you handle discipline challenges?
   (3) How do you give attention to those who do not actively seek it?

C. Lunch, In-Out Procedures, Bus Schedules
   (1) Lunchtime Problems and Victories
   (2) Coming in/Going out Procedures
   (3) Bus Students

D. Parents
   (1) Feedback
   (2) Health Records, Emergency Data
   (3) Day Care Payments

E. Ideas and Suggestions from Elementary Staff

F. Our Ideas and Suggestions

DAY CARE . . . . . . DAY CARE

By now you know we are operating a day care center for Kindergarten children. Our day care center is located in the _____ Elementary School and is serving 23 District Kindergarteners.

The children in our day care center attend _____ Kindergarten, even those who live in other areas of the district. Next year when they are in first grade, all will go to their own neighborhood school.

We feel very, very good about the loving care we are providing for our 23 day care children. Our staff is excellent and the Elementary Principal, secretaries, teachers, cafeteria workers, and custodians deserve lots of credit for being patient with us as we travel a new educational road. Thanks to everybody.

The need for day care is growing, not shrinking. We have a waiting list but as of yet, all our original day care children are still with us. There are no openings in sight.

So that we can begin planning for next year, we need to know of your needs for day care. We ask you to turn over this paper, fill out the questionnaire and return it to us by December 1. Remember, we work on a first-come, first-served basis. We number each questionnaire as it arrives in order to be totally fair to everyone.

Remember, also, that this is a questionnaire and not a promise. We'd love to promise to help you with all your child care needs but we have to study everything very carefully before beginning anything new. If we feel we can expand our day care program in a quality way, we'll do it. If we feel we can't do the very best job for children, we won't expand yet. We need your help right now. Only you can tell us what we need to know.

We need to hear from you even if you are on our waiting list.

Thanks for being our partners in our continuing quest for excellence. You are very important to us.

Let us hear from you by December 1. Send this questionnaire to school with a school-age child and save 22¢ or mail to:

Day Care Administrator
_____ School District
(Address)

DAY CARE QUESTIONNAIRE

Please answer *all* questions

(1) Is your Kindergartener in our day care program this year?

_____ Yes _____ No

If you answered "yes," would you need day care during the Summer of 19___ (this year)?

_____ Yes _____ No

(2) If your child is a Kindergartener *this year* (but is *not* in our day care center), will you need day care services during the Summer of 19___ ?

_____ Yes _____ No

(3) If your child is eligible for Kindergarten in 19___ (5 by September 30), will you need cay care services during the 19___-___ school year?

_____ Yes _____ No

(4) If you have a young elementary age child (or children), will you have a need for day care during the Summer of 19___ ?

_____ Yes _____ No

If you answered "yes," circle grade your child is in this year.

Pre-1st 1st 2nd

(5) If your child will be in *first grade* during the 19___-___ school year, are you in need of before or after school day care?

_____ Yes _____ No

_____ Before School _____ After School _____ Both

(6) If your child will be in *second grade* during the 19___-___ school year, are you in need of before or after school day care?

_____ Yes _____ No

_____ Before School _____ After School _____ Both

(7) Can you afford *approximately* $1.00 per hour for child care?

_____ Yes _____ No

(8) Are you in need of Federal assistance for child care because you are the head of a low-income family?

_____ Yes _____ No

Would you like information regarding assistance from the 3 P's program?

_____ Yes _____ No

Please write any questions or comments in this space.

PARENT'S NAME _____

CHILD'S (CHILDREN'S) NAME AND AGE _____

_____

ADDRESS _____ PHONE NO. (Home) _____

_____ (Work) _____

NEIGHBORHOOD SCHOOL _____

BACK

_____ **SCHOOL DISTRICT**

Day Care Program

Center #2

Target Date: December 19, 19___

List of Planned Equipment and Planned Room Arrangement

The following equipment will be available for day care children in the _____ Day Care Center. The children range in age between three and six.

(1) Gross motor equipment such as a balance beam, wooden blocks, wooden riding toys, and rubber balls.
(2) Easels for art work.
(3) Puzzles, games, and other manipulatives.
(4) An area carpet (9′ × 12′).
(5) Low tables and child-size chairs.
(6) Two sinks and two toilets (one for girls and one for boys).
(7) "Cubbies" and other storage equipment.
(8) Individual mats for resting or napping.

The following room arrangement is being planned:

(1) A home-like concept will guide our room arrangement. It is our desire to de-institutionalize the center so it appears to be more like "home" than school. Unanimity reigns among District educators in this regard. Philosophically, we believe a day care center should not replicate a Kindergarten classroom.
(2) A "living room" will dominate one area of the center. A sofa or two, a comfortable chair, a rocker or two, an end table, a table lamp, and a bookcase, books, and magazines will be placed in this living room area.
(3) A gross motor area will be set up along the outside wall.
(4) A "play" kitchen will be set up next to the gross motor area.
(5) A quiet play area will be created next to the living room. This area will house puzzles, art supplies, and other manipulatives emphasizing fine motor exploration. A table and chairs will be available for children who choose to use them.

Plan of Daily Activities and Routines

_____ Day Care Center #2 will be open Monday through Friday from 7 A.M. to 6:00 P.M. beginning December 19, 19___ . Twenty children will be involved in this program either full-time or part-time. The most structured part of the day will be during the morning hours. Here is our projected daily plan:

7:00 A.M. to 8:30 A.M. — Children begin arriving. They play in the quiet area, rest if they are still sleepy, and/or have juice if they need it.

8:30 A.M. to 10 A.M. — Stories, coloring, talking time, project time, crafts

FRONT

10 A.M. to 10:30 A.M.—Large muscle activities, singing, and dancing

10:30 A.M. to 11:10 A.M.—Outdoors for an enjoyable, healthy walk. Play on playground after walk. If weather is bad, children will play in center.

11:15 A.M.—Lunch—A hot lunch will be served in the cafeteria. Sixth grade students will assist the younger children.

12 noon—Rest time

1:30 P.M.—Outdoors, if weather permits.

2:30 P.M. to 3:30 P.M.—Free choice will prevail. Some children will need to rest. Others will choose to play with blocks, puzzles, and other manipulatives. Some will enjoy story time or arts and crafts projects.

Parents will begin picking up their children at intervals between 3:30 and 6 P.M.

Staff Qualifications and Functions

One certified elementary teacher will be hired by January 3, 19___ . The certified teacher will be referred to as "Group Supervisor." The four remaining staff members (formerly employed by West Lawn Day Care Center) will assist the teacher as Assistant Group Supervisor or Aides.

The certified teacher will reveal a genuine love of young children and demonstrate an applicable understanding of the needs of preschoolers. The teacher will also be able to assume leadership, supervise aides, develop lesson plans, deal warmly and effectively with parents, maintain attendance records, and compile other pertinent data.

The Assistant Group Supervisors will assume a leadership role in the absence of the certified teacher. They will carry out the plans of the Supervisor.

Aides will be hired to maintain optimal adult-child ratios.

Aides and the assistant group supervisor will express a genuine love of children and demonstrate a warmth and acceptance of others. Aides will assist the group supervisor with children's activities as well as carry out the daily plans developed by the supervisor.

Aides and the assistant group supervisor might be certified teachers. They also might be adults who did not graduate from high school. Human quality is the most important qualification of day care employees.

If we can work out transportation complexities, high school students will be taking part in our day care activities. These students will receive training as volunteer aides and will be supervised by the home economics teacher and the Early Childhood Supervisor.

A lab school concept will be attempted in our day care center. Our goal is to create an environment that is rich in positive learnings for both young children and high school students.

The Early Childhood Supervisor will be considered Director of Day Care and will oversee the curricular and staff development components of the program. The building Principal will assume day-to-day administrative duties.

BACK

101

DAY CARE

Dear Parents,

Enclosed are two day care agreements. Please sign both, keep *one* and return *one* to us as soon as possible. If you have any questions regarding this agreement, please contact us.

We are anxious to meet all of our day care parents but between the transfer from _____ Day Care to _____ Day Care and December busyness, we will have to wait until January to schedule an evening meeting. Also, by January we hope to have a new group supervisor for you to meet.

Beginning December 19 your child (or children) will be eating lunch in the _____ cafeteria. The children will receive the regular school lunch and we believe they will like this experience.

We will evaluate our new program very carefully because we accept nothing but the best for our children.

You will be receiving more information at our parent meeting in January.

Thanks for being our new partners.

Sincerely,

Early Childhood Supervisor

_____ SCHOOL DISTRICT'S DAY CARE PROGRAM AGREEMENT

I wish to register my child _____ for _____ day care program. My child's program will be in the _____ School.

My child will need day care on the following days and times:

My child's day care cost will be: _____ weekly. This fee includes lunch, snacks, and cost of materials.

My first payment is due one week in advance. If during the year I no longer need day care services, I will notify the district *one week ahead.*

If my child misses an occasional day due to a minor short-term illness, I understand I will not receive credit for these days. However, if my child has a lengthy illness, the district will attempt to work out a mutually agreeable payment plan.

I understand that day care staff salaries are paid directly from day care parents' fees. Day Care fees *must* be paid on time so that the payroll can be met and the district can meet its other expenses. If fees are not paid on their due date, I understand that my child's day care services will be terminated unless other arrangements have been made with the district.

I agree to pay a nonrefundable $10 registration fee. My $10 check is enclosed with this signed day care agreement. (Checks are made payable to _____ *District Day Care.*)

My child will begin day care on the following date: _____. I will pay for my child's day care services *one week before* he or she begins the program.

I approve my child's day care plan and agree to abide by all regulations. I will sign both copies and return one copy to the district by _____ in order to reserve a space for my child.

_____   _____   _____
Administrator's Signature   Parent's Signature   Date

April 13, 19__

TO: Superintendent and Assistant Superintendent
FROM: Early Childhood Supervisor
RE: Day Care *Staffing* and *Expenses*

If Day Care children attend P.M. Kindergarten, this is our staffing plan:

Daily Staffing

Supervisor	6:30 A.M. to 12:15 = 5¾ hrs.
1 Aide	7:00 A.M. to noon = 5 hrs.
Student Aides	8:00 A.M. to noon
1 Aide	2:00 P.M. to 5:30 = 3½ hrs.
1 Aide	2:00 P.M. to 5:30 = 3½ hrs.

Weekly Expenses

Supervisor	5¾ hrs. × 5 days = 28¾ hrs.
1 Aide	5 hrs. × 5 days = 25 hrs.
1 Aide	3½ hrs. × 5 days = 17½ hrs.
1 Aide	3½ hrs. × 5 days = 17½ hrs.
	Total Weekly Hours = 88¾ hrs.

Supervisor	29 hrs. × $6 = $174 (+ S.S., Workman's 20 Comp. & Retirement)
Aides	60 hrs. × $4 = $240
	Weekly Salaries $434

Other Expenses (Weekly)

Children's Lunches—**22 children** × $5	=	$110.00
Utilities	=	15.00
Snacks	=	25.00
Insurance	=	1.50
Materials, Supplies	=	15.00
Total other expenses		$166.50

Total Weekly Expenses

Salaries	$434.00
Other Expenses	$166.50
	$600.50

Total Weekly Income	$666.00
Total Weekly Expenses	$600.50
Weekly Reserve	$ 65.50

ENDNOTES

1. Caldwell, Bettye M., "What is Quality Child Care?" *Young Children*, p. 6 (March 1984).
2. Stevens, Joseph H., Jr., "The National Day Care Home Study," *Young Children* (May 1982).
3. Elkind, David, "Erik Erikson's Eight Ages of Man," *Sociology 82–83*, Guilford, Ct., The Dushkin Publishing Group, Inc., pp. 46 and 47 (1982).
4. Hjelle, Larry A. and Daniel J. Ziegler, *Personality Theories*, N.Y., McGraw-Hill Book Co., pp. 66–70 (1976).
5. Elkind, pp. 46 and 47.
6. Bruner, Jerome, *Under Five In Britain*, Upsilanti, Michigan, High Scope Press, pp. 71–76 (1980).
7. Bruner, pp. 61–64.
8. Bruner, pp. 64–71.
9. Ginsburg, Herbert and Sylvia Opper, *Piaget's Theory of Intellectual Development*, Prentice-Hall, Englewood Cliffs, N.J., pp. 85–94 (1969).
10. *Growing Child Research Review*, "Type of Day Care Less Important Than Quality," Volume 2, Number 7 (March 1984).
11. *Growing Child Research Review*, "Teachers, Parents Should 'Research the Research' About Early Learning," Volume 2, Number 6 (February 1984).
12. Hjelle, p. 67.
13. Elkind, pp. 46 and 47.
14. Goodman, Ellen, "A Child Is Loved, But Not Children," *Young Children*, pp. 10 and 11 (March 1982).

15. Collins, Raymond C., "Child Care and the States: The Comparative Licensing Study," *Young Children*, p. 10 (July 1983).

16. Roberts, Georgianna T., "Status and Salaries of Our Profession," *Young Children*, p. 18 (March 1983).

17. Bowlby, John, *Attachment*, Volume I, Tavistock Institute of Human Relations, p. 327 (1969).

18. Bowlby, pp. 303–304.

19. Bowlby, p. 322.

20. Bowlby, p. 209.

21. Wright, Nicolas, Editor, *Understanding Human Behavior*, Purnell Reference Books, p. 1471 (1977).

BIOGRAPHY

A late bloomer by choice, Carol M. Hoffman, wife and mother of three children, graduated summa cum laude from Kutztown University at age 33. Family is her #1 priority. Bruce has been her husband for 27 years and together they raised three perfectly wonderful children: Jill, age 25 and Ted and Tod, age 22. In addition, a loving son-in-law, Ken and a beautiful new granddaughter, Kristin Leigh, enhance family life.

In a forever sense, her mother remains her greatest influence and inspiration. As an older college student often lacking self-confidence, Dr. Walter Warzeski remains her great encourager.

Education is her second #1 priority. An educator for twelve years, she has been a Kindergarten teacher, a Title IV-C Project Director, and is presently Early Childhood Supervisor for the Wilson School District. She holds a Master's Degree from Kutztown University and Elementary Supervisory Certification from Millersville University.

Mrs. Hoffman developed early childhood programs for public schools which include monthly parent newsletters, parenting courses, preschool activities, day care, counseling and student volunteer programs for high school students.

She has had several educational articles published. She

serves as a consultant on such subjects as early childhood, school readiness, parenting, family constellation, day care in the public schools and promoting student self-discipline. She and Stanley Dubelle recently co-authored a book on discipline called *Misbehavin'*.